From the Holy Land to the New Jerusalem

Published and Forthcoming by new Academia Publishing

GOD, GREED, AND GENOCIDE: The Holocaust through the Centuries, by Arthur Grenke

FROM PIETY TO POLITICS: The Evolution of Sufi Brotherhoods, by Barbara DeGorge

NATIONALISM, HISTORIOGRAPHY, AND THE (RE)CON-STRUCTION OF THE PAST, Claire Norton, ed.

TURKEY'S MODERNIZATION: Refugees from Nazism and Atatürk's Vision, by Arnold Reisman

SLAVIC THINKERS OR THE CREATION OF POLITIES: Intellectual History and Political Thought in Central Europe and the Balkans in the 19th Century, by Josette Baer

THE INNER ADVERSARY: The Struggle against Philistinism as the Moral Mission of the Russian Intelligentsia, by Timo Vihavainen

AN ARCHITECT OF DEMOCRACY: Building a Mosaic of Peace, by James Robert Huntley

PETER STRICKLAND: New London Shipmaster, Boston Merchant, First Consul to Senegal, by Stephen H. Grant

PAN-AFRICANISM, PAN-AFRICANISTS, AND AFRICAN LIBERATION IN THE 21ST CENTURY, by Horace Campbell and Rodney Worrell

PAN-AFRICANISM IN BARBADOS: An Analysis of the Activities of the Major 20th-Century Pan-African Formations in Barbados, by Rodney Worrell

ON THE ROAD TO BAGHDAD, or TRAVELING BICULTURALISM: Theorizing a Bicultural Approach to Contemporary World Fiction, Gönul Pultar, ed.

SOCIAL PROPRIETIES: Social Relations in Early-Modern England (1500-1680), by David A. Postles

SOCIAL GEOGRAPHIES IN ENGLAND (1200-1640), by David A. Postles

To read an excerpt, visit: www.newacademia.com

From the Holy Land to the New Jerusalem

Specialness, Utopia, Holocaust

Arthur Grenke

Washington, DC

Copyright © 2008 by Arthur Grenke

New Academia Publishing, 2008

All rights reserved. No part of this book may be reproduced or transmitted in any form or by any means, electronic or mechanical, including photocopying, recording, or by any information storage and retrieval system.

Printed in the United States of America

Library of Congress Control Number: 2007926536
ISBN 978-0-9787713-7-9 paperback (alk. paper)

New Academia Publishing, LLC
P.O. Box 27420- Washington, DC 20038-7420
info@newacademia.com
www.newacademia.com

Contents

Preface vii

Introduction 1

PART I HOLY LAND AND HOLOCAUST 15
1. Holy Land and the Destruction of the Idolaters 17
2. Armageddon and the Creation of the New Jerusalem 31

PART II EVENTS AND THE RECORD THEREOF 43
3. A Chronology of Israelite History 45
4. Recording Historical Events 53
5. Reward and Punishment and God's Relationship with Israel 69
6. Changes in the Israelite View of the Messiah or Savior, and the Progression from the Holy Land to the New Jerusalem 85
7. The Historical Experience, Reward and Punishment, and the Savior 93
8. From Earthly Event to Apocalyptic Vision—An Evolution of Beliefs and Concepts 97
Conclusion 113

Notes 129
Bibliography 138
Index 142

Preface

From the Holy Land to the New Jerusalem evolved while I was examining the nature of the holocaust and the dynamics leading to it. The issue arose in the mid-1980s, when our local school board decided to introduce holocaust studies into the Ottawa school curriculum. Members of the Jewish community argued that only their experiences in Nazi Germany should be examined as only they had suffered what can be called a holocaust. Members of other communities, in turn, argued that they had also suffered a holocaust and that their experiences could also teach something to future generations.

The dispute raised certain questions in my mind. I couldn't help wondering: what exactly is a holocaust? What are the dynamics contributing to this type of genocide? To answer these questions, I examined different genocides, from the past to the present, which researchers had called holocausts. Thus, I looked at the destruction of the idolaters, mentioned in the Old Testament, the persecution of the witches in the Middle Ages, and concluded with the mass destructions carried out by the Khmer Rouge in Cambodia in the 1970s. The study was published in 2005 by New Academia Publishing, under the title *God, Greed, and Genocide: The Holocaust through the Centuries*. It has also been translated into German, by Herbig Verlag. Published in 2005, it is available under the title *Völkermord: Weltgeschichte des Genozids*.

As I explored the destruction of the idolaters, described near the beginning of the biblical record, I was struck by the similarity between this case and the ideal existence promised to believers in the Book of Revelation, at the end of the Bible. In both cases, a particular group of elect is promised salvation. In the one case, they are promised an environment in the Holy Land that is the next best thing to Paradise. However, to assure that they will not deviate from the way of the Lord and thus be punished rather than rewarded, the Lord demanded that former inhabitants of the land be totally eliminated. As a result, an intense effort was undertaken to destroy them. In the case of the Book of Revelation, the enemy will not be killed but rather sent to hell.

Of course, the term "holocaust" was applied to the Nazi destruction of European Jewry because the Jews were targeted for total destruction. The emphasis on total destruction or elimination of the target group is seen to be the prime characteristic of the holocaust type of genocide. While the destruction of the idolaters in ancient Palestine constituted a holocaust and the destruction of sinners at the end of time promises to be a holocaust, the manner in which the elect attain salvation is quite different in these cases. The consequences are also different for the targeted enemies. In the one case, the enemies are for the most part killed; in the other case, their final destiny is hell and eternal punishment. In the one case, an ideal existence is promised in this life; in the other case, it is promised after death. In the first part of the Bible, God in many ways acts like the warrior god of other peoples. That is, he advises his chosen on how best to fight battles so as to attain victory. At the end of the Bible, God attains victory for the chosen, not through people as we know them, but through the Lamb of God. I couldn't help asking: how do we get from one scenario of salvation and destruction to the other? How do we get from the promise of utopia in the Holy Land at the beginning of the Bible to the ideal existence in heaven at the end of the Bible? How do we get from, what is to the best of my knowledge, the first holocaust in recorded history to the prophetic vision of a holocaust at the end of the Bible that will put an end to the world as we know it?

Of course, some of these questions had been with me since early childhood. I had been raised Baptist. The concepts of heaven and hell had been an integral part of my education. Bible study focused on how to avoid one and attain the other. Nevertheless, I didn't give these ideas much thought until I undertook a more detailed analysis of the destruction of the idolaters as described in the Old Testament. It made me think about the nature of the biblical message and what it says about God and humanity. It made me wonder about how we arrived at the concepts of salvation as found in the Bible, and their relationship to the Holy Land and to heaven and hell. *From the Holy Land to the New Jerusalem* is an attempt to find answers for myself. Perhaps my research may also be helpful to others who are asking similar questions.

Arthur Grenke

Introduction

In both Judaism and Christianity there is a close relationship between utopia and holocaust. This is nowhere more evident than when one looks at the paradise-like existence promised to the Israelites in the Holy Land, at the beginning of the Bible, and the blessed existence promised to believers in the Book of Revelation at the end of the Bible. In the case of the Holy Land, God's promise of the idealized life for the Israelites is closely connected to His command that the idolaters be totally destroyed. In the case of heaven and the New Jerusalem, the promise of an ideal existence for the elect is an integral part of evildoers being condemned and sent to hell. In either case, the ideal leaves no room for its opposite. In the following text, I will explore how, in the biblical account, we progress from the Holy Land at the beginning of the Bible to the heaven and hell envisioned in the Book of Revelation at its end.

Before proceeding, it may be useful to define my terms. By "utopia," I mean an idealized existence found in the perfect society, in the perfect state of being. This may be the best possible society, or state of being, on earth. It may also involve a vision of the absolutely perfect society or state of being, which, although not possible in the world as we find it, is seen as having been possible in some past state of existence, or being possible in some future state of existence. In both the case of the Holy Land and the New Jerusalem, the dreams of utopia are not an end in themselves, but are also means of avoiding destruction (in the case of the Holy Land) or the fires of hell (in the case of the New Jerusalem). In this respect, utopia also becomes a means of salvation.

Salvation and utopia are in both of these cases closely connected to the total elimination of vilified groups. In the case of the Holy Land, God commands that they all be killed. In the case of the Armageddon and the final realization of the ideal existence for the elect in heaven or the New Jerusalem, evildoers are eliminated from earth and sent down to hell where they will be punished forever. In other words, these groups suffer what has come to be identified as a "holocaust." Developed in the context of ancient Greek religious practices, the term "holocaust" means to bring a burnt offering, or to be offered as a whole burnt offering.[1] Chamoux gives some idea as to the meaning of this word as it was used to describe a particular religious ritual when he writes that in Hellenic polytheism the gods were divided into two broad categories: the gods of the sky (*uranian*) and the gods of the underworld (*chthonian*). The gods of the sky were considered to be helpful to humankind and those of the underworld maleficent. Worshippers consequently partook in sacrifices to the deities of the sky and shared the flesh of the victim, while in the *chthonian* sacrifice, offered to dangerous gods, the entire sacrifice was offered to the divinity, with the entire sacrificial offering being consumed by fire.[2]

Thus, the term "holocaust" essentially referred to a burnt offering that involved the total consumption by fire of the sacrifice being offered to the gods. It was part of a religious ritual intended to placate a deity, which in turn would permit a community to avert danger and find harmony with the universal order. It involved the sacrifice of one being so that another could draw on the benefits promised by the force or forces that controlled the fate of humankind.

The term has been applied to different cases of mass destruction that involved the creation of an ideal environment for a specific group of peoples. Thus, B.W. Anderson applies the term to describe mass destructions carried out by the early Israelites in their endeavour to dedicate their territorial base to their tribal God, Yahweh,[3] and thereby create an environment in which they would be assured of God's blessings. The term was applied to the destruction of witches in late Medieval Europe as Christian authorities sought to protect Christians against the onslaught of Satan, and thereby save Christendom from the fires of hell.[4] The term was applied to the destruction of Ukrainian farmers under Stalin when he targeted them as enemies who were thwarting his efforts to turn the Soviet Union into a proletarian utopia.[5] It was applied to Hitler's attempt to eliminate European Jewry as he sought to achieve Germany's salvation through transforming it into a tribal society.[6] In all these cases a particular group was targeted as an enemy that had to be eliminated so as to achieve the well-being of a group that saw itself as elect or special.

This drive to destroy a group so as to achieve the well-being of another is nowhere more clearly enunciated than in the command of God to the Israelites, when He states that, in the cities that He grants to them as their inheritance, they "shall let nothing that breathes remain alive, but you shall utterly destroy them: the Hittite and the Amorite and the Canaanite and the Perizzite and the Hivite and the Jebusite, just as the Lord your God has commanded you, lest they teach you according to all their abominations which they have done for their gods, and you sin against the Lord your God." (Deut. 20: 16-18). Sinning against the Lord, of course, would result in the Israelites being punished rather than rewarded, rewarded so abundantly that in the Holy Land they would enjoy the next best thing to Paradise.

Paradise, as depicted in the Book of Genesis, showed two people, the father and mother of humankind, Adam and Eve, living under blessed conditions. They had no need for clothes. They suffered neither disease nor death. They both lived off the bountifulness of nature in the Garden of Eden, where God walked with them. This blessed situation was conditional upon their keeping God's commandment. It was terminated with their breaking God's commandment, upon which they were expelled into the world as we know it.

While founded in the world as we know it, the Holy Land was to offer the Israelites some of the conditions approximating Paradise. As in the case of Paradise, these conditions were to be granted to them only if they abided by the laws of God, as handed to them through the Laws of Moses. Should they do so, their fields would be fruitful, their livestock would multiply, and health and a good life would be theirs. They would be blessed above all other peoples. Deviation from the laws, however, would lead to God turning against them and punishing them, as Adam and Eve had been punished for their disobedience.

In addition to differences in the conditions under which people lived, there are also significant differences in the way in which Paradise and the Holy Land were founded. In regard to Paradise, the Book of Genesis suggests that this was a way of life God had intended for people if they remained in harmony with His laws. The Holy Land, on the other hand, was established through war, with the deity actively participating in the attempt to totally destroy the adherents of other deities so as to certify that the people He especially loved and had chosen as His own would not be tempted to fall away from Him and thereby incur His punishment rather than His blessing. The Book of Joshua and part of Deuteronomy describe how the early Israelites carried out God's command. That is, they describe the slaughter of the idolaters on the territory selected for the worship of Israel's tribal deity.

In the Book of Revelation, at the end of the Bible, the holocaust does not so much involve people being killed as their being sent to hell and eternal perdition. In this case, the writer John, in exile on the island of Patmos, envisages massive battles in which Christ the Lamb, representing the power and vitality of God, enters into battle against the forces of evil, of Satan, "Lucifer." In this case, people may be killed. However, their death is only temporary. Let me explain. In John's view, wicked people on earth, spurred on by the source of all evil, Satan, continually foil the good deeds aspired to by the followers of Christ. In fact, they do worse; they persecute the followers of Christ. Such persecution, according to John, will continue until the end of time, or until the return of Christ, who then will do battle against the anti-Christ and all the forces of evil allied with him. Rivers of blood will be spilled and Satan and his forces will eventually be vanquished. This, however, will not bring about the final containment of evil, which will come following the day of judgement when all people, including those who have died, will be judged. After that, all who have done evil will be cast into hell with Satan, whom they had served while alive. Here they will be punished forever. The followers of Christ, however, will go to heaven and eternal bliss.

As in the case of the Holy Land, the destruction of one group is intricately linked with the ideal existence to be attained by another, with the attainment of heaven being an integral part of the elimination of the wicked. The destruction of the wicked, together with the creation of a new heaven and a new earth, are part and parcel of a process leading to the salvation of those who are adherents of the true religion. It will be part of the destruction of the old world and the creation of the New Jerusalem that would be inhabited forever by all those who have been purified by the blood of the Lamb, who have chosen Christ as their savior, who are adherents of the true faith. The wicked, on the other hand, will be sent down to hell and eternal punishment.

The purpose of this work is to explore how we get from Joshua as savior to Christ as savior; to explore how we get from the ideal existence promised in the Holy Land to the blessed state promised to true believers in heaven and the New Jerusalem. To trace this progression, I will use primarily the biblical text to guide my exploration. My main reason for doing so is to avoid becoming involved in the ongoing controversy concerning to what extent the biblical record is myth and to what extent it is literal truth. People who believe the latter are generally described as fundamentalist Christians. The former view is increasingly being forwarded in particular by biblical archaeologists who seek to relegate the Bible to myth and to write the history of the Holy Land based on the archaeological artefact.[7]

To provide the reader with an insight into the nature of the debate, I will briefly explore some of the issues raised. Doing so will give the reader an insight into my own approach and my reasons for adopting it. To begin, it would be helpful to mention that the biblical narrative of the Israelite conquest of ancient Palestine was written down several centuries after the event. It would be logical to assume, therefore, that the account was condensed and altered as it was orally passed from generation to generation. Also, somewhat different accounts of the Israelite conquest would, no doubt, have emerged over time. Thus we find that the Book of Judges presents a somewhat different version of the Israelite conquest of biblical Palestine than do other books in the Old Testament. Albrecht Alt and the German school of biblical scholars concluded from the different accounts presented in the Bible that there was no military conquest of Canaan by the Israelites, but rather a gradual and pacific penetration.[8] Other biblical scholars took issue with Alt's interpretation. This was true in particular of William Albright, who, as leader of what came to be known as the biblical archaeology movement, was convinced he could settle the issue by applying what he saw as the scientifically rigorous methods of archaeological research to biblical scholarship.[9]

Ever since modern topographical research methods began to be used in archaeological studies more than a century ago, scholars have endeavoured to locate the cities the Bible mentions as having been destroyed by Joshua and to identify the "destruction layers" from the twelfth and thirteenth centuries BC that might be attributed to the Israelite conquest. Albright and his followers adopted almost exclusively the conquest model presented in the Book of Joshua.[10] Albright's basic premise was that the Bible's account was correct and that all he had to do was find evidence of the different cities destroyed in ancient Palestine and date them. He would thereby prove the historical accuracy of the biblical record. Albright found much evidence to support the account rendered by the Book of Joshua.[11] Archaeologists such as G. Ernest Wright, John Bright, and Yigael Yadin, who shared Albright's objectives, also found evidence supporting the view that the Book of Joshua presents a fairly accurate account of events. On the basis of his findings, Yigael Yadin argued that the biblical narrative, in its broad outline, tells us that, during a certain period, the nomad Israelites attacked the city-states organization of the Holy Land and destroyed many of its cities. They set them on fire and slowly replaced them with new unfortified cities. However, they were unable to dislodge certain cities, which continued to exist in the midst of the invaders.[12]

The same conclusion was reached by scholars such as Craigie, who sought to bring together the biblical with the archaeological record. Craigie takes the view that the results of archaeological work may illuminate the background of the biblical story, filling in the gaps in the text.[13] This view is also expressed by Baez-Camargo, who argues that traditional views of the Israelite conquest of Canaan as a single, extensive campaign led by Joshua have been called into question by scholars who use the archaeological record to explore the biblical narrative. The increasingly accepted theory is that the Israelite invasion followed two main routes: one from the south, for which archaeological evidence is somewhat uncertain, and the other through the east (led by Joshua, and best described by the biblical account), across the Jordan and then towards the north.[14]

From the mid-1920s to the 1970s, Albright's approach to biblical criticism held a dominant position, particularly in North

America, where his views regarding the historicity of the Book of Joshua tended to be broadly accepted. Thereafter, a new generation of archaeologists gained prominence, which was inclined to reject Albright's view that archaeology was somehow the handmaiden of biblical scholarship, relegated to the task of expanding on the biblical record. Nor were they interested in exploring the massive destructions on which Albright and his group concentrated, but rather sought to examine the archaeological record of everyday life.

Building on findings of archaeologists who take issue with Albright and his school, William Dever proceeds to construct his own theory as to the historicity of the Book of Joshua and the origins of Israel.[15] He argues that the biblical account in the Book of Joshua may have come down to us as a record of the "house of Joseph." He adds that "these newcomers" to Canaan may have passed through Transjordan, entered Canaan via Jericho, and "intruded forcefully" into central Palestine. Such a route would explain some of the conquest narratives in the Book of Joshua. He goes on to say that, in time, the story of the house of Joseph became the story of "all Israel" because it was the only extant record. As an illustration, he suggests that the landing of the *Mayflower* might have become the story of all Americans if it had been the only record retained relating to the landing of Europeans in America.[16]

The landing of the *Mayflower* is not a mere story but is based in fact. Applying Dever's analogy to the Book of Joshua suggests that the biblical accounts of these conquests are also not mere stories but also have a basis in fact. From this perspective, Dever's account is not all that different from that of Craigie or Baez-Camargo, who argue that different tribal groups contributed to the biblical record and that, in its broad outline, the archaeological record essentially supports the account presented in the Book of Joshua. Of course, Dever calls these accounts mere "origin stories," written to show Yahweh's work on behalf of His people.[17] He does not seek to resolve the question of the extent to which these stories are factual. At the same time, he does admit that it is difficult for archaeologists to ascertain the belief systems of ancient peoples and that archaeologists are not equipped to be palaeo-theologians.

Dever has not been the only one drawing particularly on archaeological evidence to discount or improve upon the biblical record.[18] Among scholars working in the field, one of the most analytically rigorous has probably been Israel Finkelstein, who in *The Bible Unearthed* shows quite convincingly that the original creators of the biblical narrative were wrong on numerous occasions in identifying the location where the destructions mentioned in the Bible occurred. They were often wrong in identifying the time of these destructions. Also, in many of their accounts they overemphasized the significance of a particular person or event. Furthermore, creators of the biblical record were very much influenced by the environment in which they found themselves, by their religious beliefs, and by the aspirations of rulers and religious leaders at the time when the Bible was committed to written form.[19]

Finkelstein not only criticizes the biblical record, but also presents his own account of how the Holy Land was established. Dismissing the biblical account of the conquest, Finkelstein suggests various alternatives: Sea People caused the destructions mentioned in the Bible; or they were the result of an Egyptian invasion. In a footnote he mentions that they may have been caused by the Israelites.

This does not, of course, discredit the essentials of the biblical account. From the evidence Finkelstein presents, one could well conclude that the people who created the written record were very poor at dating events. Thus, the Israelite attack on Canaanite cities could well have occurred at the time when the Sea People attacked and destroyed the Hittite Empire and weakened Egypt's hold over Canaan. Furthermore, he focuses on the Sea People or perhaps the Egyptians using military force to assert their dominance. He further suggests that the Israelites, who in his view were Canaanites who were monotheists, moved into a position where they dominated at least part of the area without going to war. This doesn't tell us how and why a monotheist monarchy came to power. Nor does it correspond to what we know of the manner in which other groups gained dominance in a particular area in the past. Power and the use of force tend to be fairly universal. The biblical record tells us that force was used to assert monotheist dominance. Thus, one could well argue that the evidence Finkelstein presents to support his argument gives more credence to many parts of the biblical record rather than proves his case.

Nor does ignoring the ban,[20] as Finkelstein does, abolish the problems the extensive discussions of it, in particular in the early part of the Bible, raise for his account. If the ban was the result of a creative flash of insight by a writer of the account, what inspired it? The suggestion that it may have arisen as a possible solution to avoiding the experiences Israel had undergone isn't sufficient. Why would it arise at a time when Judah's main enemies were using expulsion rather than mass destruction as a means of sustaining their power? Why would Josiah, the king of Judah, advocate so extreme a solution at the time when he was himself in danger of losing his kingdom? If creators of the biblical account were the cynics Finkelstein often suggests, would they want to put such ideas into the mind of their enemies?

In any case, the reforms King Josiah undertook are a far cry from the destruction evident in the ban described in the first part of the Bible. The fact that he could undertake these changes without significant protest suggests that they were in keeping with an older, stronger tradition. Furthermore, the Bible has a much more satisfactory timing of these ideas and/or events than is suggested by Finkelstein. They occurred during the early period, when the idea of sacrificing conquered peoples to the gods would have been significantly more acceptable than it was at the time of Josiah. At the same time, the Bible also presents an idea of when the ancient Israelites gave up the ban and used other means to deal with the original inhabitants of the land. The biblical account, as such, has a greater inherent logic than is evident in Finkelstein's account.

Finkelstein remarks that the Jews at first differentiated themselves from other peoples by not eating pork,[21] and suggests that this later evolved into a full religion. This doesn't tell us how dietary laws led to a coherent religious outlook different from those of Judah's neighbours. Also, while Finkelstein's comment is interesting, it doesn't reflect at all the pattern whereby we have seen other major religions develop. No matter whether we look at Christianity, Islam, Buddhism, or Zoroastrianism, for example, these all involved a charismatic leader, a leader who spelled out certain principles and encouraged people to abide by them. In this respect, the accounts we have about the roles of Moses or of Joshua present a picture in the development of Judaism that is much more in keeping with our observations of the way other religions developed than is Finkelstein's account. In fact, Josiah's reforms make much more sense when looked at, not in terms of his essentially creating a new religion, but in terms of the whole biblical story of people accepting a particular religion, of gradually falling away from it and then being brought back through radical religious reforms.

Also, archaeology doesn't provide all the answers and, in fact, at times raises questions rather than provides answers. An example is the First Temple, the existence of which Finkelstein admits to, despite the lack of archaeological evidence for it.[22] I would argue that there is good reason to conclude that the role of war and the ban in the conquest of the Holy Land also can fit into this category. The numerous destructions many of these centres underwent, as well as the manner in which recorders of the biblical account created the record, as we know it, would point in that direction.

Furthermore, in the Bible we have observations on social customs, religious practices, and on other aspects of the life of the early Israelites. The presence of these details can hardly be explained in an account that, as Finkelstein suggests, was created essentially to further the territorial interests of Judah and the dynastic objectives of its monarchy.

Problems are also evident in other areas of the accounts presented by archaeologists such as Finkelstein. They show up in the questionable assumptions they make at different times and in the evidence they accept and reject. They appear in arguments one archaeologist makes to prove his point only to have another archaeologist, coming from a different perspective, using different data or even the same data, prove him wrong.

Both Dever's and Finkelstein's accounts demonstrate that although archaeology has been quite successful in pointing out shortcomings of the Bible as history, it has been less successful in presenting a satisfactory alternative account on the establishment of the Holy Land. In part, this stems from the archaeological method itself. Dark argues that the material past does not speak for itself; it speaks only through the beliefs, ideas, and frame of reference of the archaeologist.[23] Commenting on the usefulness of archaeology in Bible criticism, Boling states that what archaeology can do for biblical study is provide a physical context in time and place. Inscriptions and other evidence are of exceptional importance for the biblical background and for the occasional mention of biblical places and names. The remainder of the archaeological record, however, leaves room for interpretation, which is very much influenced by the beliefs and attitudes of the people doing the interpreting.[24]

Furthermore, although archaeology can provide us with considerable information on the material past as this relates to the Bible, it has been less successful in providing us with information on the beliefs of the ancient Hebrews. For this, the main source is the Bible, which reflects the religious beliefs of the people who left us this record and their views regarding the role Yahweh played in the life of His people. Boling informs us that, when writing the Book of Joshua, the writers drew on a variety of older sources.[25] This could help explain why we find different and, at times, seemingly contradictory accounts of the conquest. Nor are such contradictions necessarily a denial that the conquest described in the Book of Joshua has a basis in fact. To reach a conclusion in this regard, it would probably be more sensible to look at the overall biblical account. This suggests that the events described in the Book of Joshua constituted, not an isolated incident, but part of Israelite practice for a prolonged period.[26]

Craigie argues that if the historian's task were simply to resolve the tension inherent in the biblical narrative, it could be argued that the Books of Joshua and Judges give complementary, but considerably oversimplified, pictures of the history of the Hebrew conquest and settlement. The Book of Joshua provides an overview of a major military campaign that brought the Israelites into the Promised Land. At the same time, however, Hebrew control was restricted to a few areas. The summary and the beginning of Judges and the narratives that follow present an account of a more prolonged period of consolidation after the initial conquest.[27]

What concerns us in this study is not only the chronological record but also the motives of the people who "intruded forcefully" into biblical Palestine. Although written from the perspective of the belief system of the people of the time, the Book of Joshua provides us with an insight into the objectives of these invaders. The scriptural account informs us that their goal was to slaughter all the people who did not believe in Yahweh and were not members of the Tribes of Israel. Although we cannot ascertain from either the biblical or the archaeological record to what extent the invaders followed these directives, we can say that, from the evidence they had, the writers of the Book of Joshua concluded that the invaders had followed these directives. We are also informed as to why they followed these directives: they saw in this a way of ensuring that the Israelites would receive the blessings of Yahweh and avoid His punishment.

This does not mean that they were totally accurate in their presentation. The archaeological evidence is persuasive enough to convince us that these accounts were very much influenced by the beliefs of the people who prepared them and by the social conditions under which they were prepared. At the same time, the archaeological evidence suggests that the writers of the biblical account brought together events that occurred at different times, attributing them to the actions of a major, decisive leader acting under God's guidance. Such focussing and magnification are probably natural for an orally transmitted record. Despite these shortcomings, the evidence strongly suggests that war and the ban had a role in establishing monotheism in what came to be called the Holy Land.

There is good reason to believe, therefore, that the holocaust described in Deuteronomy and the Book of Joshua has some basis in the historical past, expressing the aspiration of Israelites of the time. However, this past was interpreted in the light of the Jewish faith and with the purpose of perpetuating this faith. By contrast, the Bible makes quite clear that the mass destructions described in the Book of Revelation never happened. At the same time, the biblical record also shows that this envisaged destruction evolved from the historical experience of the Israelites. It grew out of the aspiration of the Hebrew community to realize the promise they saw God having given unto them as His special elect.

The question this study poses is: how, in the Bible, do we get from the destruction of the idolaters and the establishment of Israel in the Holy Land to the destruction of sinners and the establishment of the New Jerusalem in heaven? There is a considerable distance between the two. That is, one is part of God's choice to be the God of Israel, to care for the children of Israel as

Introduction 13

a special people. It is part and parcel of the Israelites' attempt to create a special environment on earth where they could best serve their God and in turn enjoy the next best thing to Paradise.

The concept of the New Jerusalem is an essential part of creating a world in which the elect will forever be able to serve God. They would no longer be harassed and misled from the way of the Lord either by Satan or by the presence of evildoers in their midst. Rather, they would be initiated into a world where there is no temptation, a world void of corruptness. In order to attain this level of purity, all corruptness will be totally eliminated from the realm to be occupied by the elect. The people and spirits who are the cause of the corruptness will not die but, rather, will be sent to hell, where they will be punished forever.

To explore the progression in the Bible from one ideal state to another, from one holocaust to another, I will commence by presenting a summary of the biblical account relating the destruction of the idolaters. Following this, I will do the same with the Book of Revelation, illustrating the relationship between the destruction of non-believers, of Armageddon, and the creation of the New Earth and the New Jerusalem, the ideal world for Christian believers.

Following this, I will explore influences that may have caused recorders of the biblical record to speak of a Paradise-like existence in time and space, in the earthly domain, in the case of the first holocaust, and of salvation after death and in the eternal sphere, in the case of the holocaust that would put an end to the world as we know it. Basic to either case is the human relationship to God, in particular God's use of reward and punishment to influence people's behaviour. In this regard, a reward may be seen as something that is valued being earned by a person or groups for behaviour that is approved of by the person or entity judging this behaviour. By punishment, I mean negative consequences ensuing from this evaluation. In both these instances, the entity judging the behaviour is God, or Yahweh, who is seen to be the universal and only true God in the universe.

As both reward and punishment tell us something about humankind and God as depicted in the Bible, I shall seek to give an idea as to how each is presented in the biblical record. I shall explore different ways in which God uses reward and punishment to influence people's behaviour. At the same time, I will seek to explore the manner in which the biblical record was created and how this contributed to the evolution of ideas and concepts found therein.

Also, I will explore the idea of the savior as developed in the biblical text. For example, in the Book of Joshua, the Israelite leader gives evidence of possessing few supernatural powers. His power lies in his ability to persuade the tribal deity, Yahweh, to war on behalf of his people. The deity responds in marvellous ways. Joshua himself, however, remains human in every sense of the word as he goes about destroying the idolaters so as to establish a locale on earth where the Israelites could enjoy the blessings of Yahweh. In the Book of Revelation, at the end of the Bible, we have Christ the Savior, the Son of God, doing battle with the Anti-Christ and the forces of evil allied with him. Both Christ and Satan in this context are supernatural forces beyond our everyday ken. The battles they fight take place in heaven as well as on earth. The saints, consisting for the most part of dead people who during their life had accepted Christ as their savior, will join the angels in heaven to worship God. Satan and his followers, consisting of resurrected evildoers and evildoers who are still alive, will be banished to hell where they will suffer eternal punishment. The struggle as well as rewards and punishment are beyond our everyday experiences and can only be imagined.

The objective of this study is to shed light on the nature of the relationship between the promises of an ideal existence for the Israelites and the destruction of the idolaters at the beginning of the Bible, and the rewards offered true believers and corresponding punishment to be handed out to non-believers, as described in the Book of Revelation. In doing so, the study gives evidence of how a community alters itself to adapt basic elements of its belief system to the ever-changing circumstances of its environment. Significantly, it provides an insight into how efforts by Jewish religious leaders to sustain basic elements of their faith laid the basis for Christianity, and with it a vision of the ideal existence radically different from that of traditional Judaism.

Part I

Holy Land and Holocaust

1
Holy Land and the Destruction of Idolaters

God's Command

The first holocaust occurred in the temporal sphere and involved the destruction of the idolaters so as to create an ideal environment for the people of Israel in what came to be called the "Holy Land." In some respects, this destruction was unique. At the same time, it ensued from a god-centered belief system that characterized all ancient societies. However, unlike other societies in the ancient Middle East, which were polytheistic and worshipped a number of gods, the Israelites were monotheistic, worshipping only one deity, Yahweh, whom they saw as the only true God, other deities being either mere objects of wood or stone, or false gods. In many respects, the destruction of the idolaters came about as a result of the Israelite attempt to attain the rewards and avoid the punishment of this one true God.

Like other ancients, the Israelites lived in a mythological universe, a universe ruled by God or the gods. Supernatural deities were seen to control all areas of personal and community life. They bequeathed good health or caused sickness, influenced the weather, and determined fruitfulness. In wars, they supported one community of believers against enemies who usually had other gods. In other words, in ancient times humans perceived the gods as having a central role in determining the well being of the individual and of the community of which he or she was a member. Religious sacrifices and other means of homage were intended to avoid punishment and solicit the support of the supernatural world, enabling the individual and the community to lead a successful existence.

In most instances, deities were associated with a hill, a mountain, or with some other locale that by its very nature expressed to worshippers some dimension of the divine. As well, political units, such as city-states, also had their deities. As city-states expanded, often into empires controlling a number of states or an entire region, the conquering cities tended to absorb the deities of other city-states. Under these conditions, the gods tended to find themselves ranked in importance. Thus, in ancient Babylon, for example, the main deity tended to be Marduk, who, as the traditional Babylonian deity, was given preference by most Babylonian rulers. Citizens, while expected to give obeisance to whomever was chosen as the main deity by the ruler, were also permitted to have their own pantheon of deities to serve their particular needs.

The case was quite different for the Israelites. They viewed the Israelite deity, Yahweh, not merely as the only true deity, with all other deities being mere objects of wood or stone, but also saw these false gods as tempters seeking to win the Israelites away from the worship of their God. Believing in many deities, most ancient conquerors were inclined to permit conquered peoples to continue in the worship of their gods. In fact, they did more. When taking over a territory whose inhabitants worshipped different gods, the conquerors tended to absorb these gods into their pantheon, so as to enable them to recruit their support in the pursuit of their goals.

The Israelite belief system, however, did not allow for this. Unlike societies with many gods, Israelite society saw itself as threatened by the absorption of other gods and other belief systems, essentially because the Israelite God, Yahweh, was seen as punishing people He had chosen as His possession for worshipping other gods. He demanded the destruction of all altars built to these gods. Not only that, He demanded that the Israelites destroy all worshippers of these gods in the Holy Land, territory He had chosen as His own, so that these people would not lead the Israelites into worshipping false gods, and, through this, be punished rather than rewarded. In many respects, the destruction resulting from this might be seen as a sacrifice to consecrate the land the God Yahweh had chosen for His people. At the same time, the slaughter was carried out to certify that, rather than be punished by their deity, the Israelites would be assured of the best life possible on earth. Thus we read:

Holy Land and the Destruction of Idolaters

For you are holy people to the LORD your God; the LORD your God has chosen you to be a people for Himself, a special treasure above all the peoples on the face of the earth. The LORD did not set His love on you nor choose you because you were more in number than any other people, for you were the least of all peoples; but because the LORD loves you, and because He would keep the oath which He swore to your fathers, the LORD has brought you out with a mighty hand, and redeemed you from the house of bondage, from the hand of Pharaoh king of Egypt. Therefore know that the LORD your God, He is God, the faithful God who keeps covenant and mercy for a thousand generations with those who love Him and keep His commandments, and He repays those who hate Him to their face, to destroy them. He will not be slack with him who hates Him; He will repay him to his face. Therefore you shall keep the commandments, the statutes, and the judgments which I command you today, to observe them. Then it shall come to pass, because you listen to these judgments, and keep and do them, that the LORD your God will keep with you the covenant and the mercy which He swore to your fathers. And He will love you and bless you and multiply you; He will also bless the fruit of your womb and the fruit of your land, your grain and your new wine and your oil, the increase of your cattle and the offspring of your flock, in the land of which He swore to your fathers to give you. You shall be blessed above all peoples; there shall not be male or female barren among you or among your livestock. And the LORD will take away from you all sickness; and will afflict you with none of the terrible diseases of Egypt which you have known, but will lay them on all those who hate you. Also you shall destroy all the peoples whom the LORD your God delivers over to you; your eye shall have no pity on them; nor shall you serve their gods, for that will be a snare to you. (Deut. 7: 6-16)

The Destruction

The biblical record of the destruction of the idolaters serves essentially to demonstrate the power of the Israelite deity to go into battle on behalf of His people so as to establish the Holy Land, the land where only He would be worshipped. The account opens with the Israelite attack on Jericho (Josh. 6:15-24), a major fortified city blocking the Israelite penetration and conquest of ancient Palestine. We find the people of Jericho safe behind the walls of their city, with the Israelites, who had become a nomadic desert people following their flight from Egypt, unable to take the city until their God, Yahweh, advised them to march around the city seven times. At the seventh time, after the priests had blown their trumpets, the people of Israel shouted, upon which the city walls fell flat and the invaders poured into the stronghold, upon which they slaughtered all the inhabitants except for the prostitute Rahab and her family, who were spared as a reward for her betraying her people to the invaders.

In the case of the conquest of Ai, the Israelite God acted more in a capacity as adviser. He counseled the Israelite leader, Joshua, on where to position his troops, to camp the fighting men on the north side of Ai, and to take about five thousand men, and set them in ambush between Bethel and Ai, to the west of the city. Unaware of the troops waiting in ambush, the king of Ai and his warriors hurried to meet the main body of Israelites in combat. Once the fighters of Ai had left the city, Joshua, on the advice of his God, signaled for the troops waiting in ambush to attack. Thereupon, the ambush broke into the city and set it on fire. Caught between the Israelite main force and the men in ambush who had set the city on fire, the fighters of Ai were decimated. After this, the Israelite invaders turned upon the women and children, destroying them as well.

In the case of Hazor, one of the most important cities conquered by Joshua, the Israelites at first hesitated to attack it, because they were vastly outnumbered. However, the Lord counseled Joshua not to be afraid of this multitude of soldiers, for He would deliver them all into the hands of the Israelites. When Joshua and his men of war attacked the next day, the Lord gave victory to the Israelites, who destroyed the defenders of Hazor to the last man. Following this, the Israelites took the city, and "struck all the people who were in it with the edge of the sword, utterly destroying them. There was none left breathing. Then he (Joshua) burned Hazor with fire" (Josh. 11:11).

Following the description of the conquest and destruction of some of the major centers, or centers where the support of the Lord fighting on behalf of Israel was especially evident, the Book of Joshua presents a summarized account of the destruction of other locales. Thus, we read:

> On that day Joshua took Makkedah, and struck it and its king with the edge of the sword. He utterly destroyed them – all the people who were in it. He let none remain. He also did to the king of Makkedah as he had done to the king of Jericho.
>
> Then Joshua passed from Makkedah, and all Israel with him, to Libnah; and fought against Libnah. And the LORD also delivered it and its king into the hand of Israel; he struck it and all the people who were in it with the edge of the sword. He let none remain in it, but did to its king as he had done to the king of Jericho.
>
> Then Joshua passed from Libnah, and all Israel with him, to Lachish, and they encamped against it and fought against it. And the LORD delivered Lachish into the hand of Israel, who took it on the second day, and struck it and all the people who were in it with the edge of the sword, according to all that he had done to Libnah.
>
> Then Horam king of Gezer came up to help Lachish; and Joshua struck him and his people, until he left him none remaining.
>
> From Lachish Joshua passed to Eglon, and all Israel with him; and they encamped against it and fought against it. They took it on that day and struck it with the edge of the sword; all the people who were in it he utterly destroyed that day, according to all that he had done to Lachish.
>
> So Joshua went up from Eglon, and all Israel with him, to Hebron; and they fought against it. And took it and struck it with the edge of the sword - its king, all its cities, and all the people who were in it; he left none

remaining, according to all that he had done to Eglon, but utterly destroyed it and all the people who were in it.

Then Joshua returned, and all Israel with him, to Debir, and they fought against it. And he took it and its king and all its cities; they struck them with the edge of the sword and utterly destroyed all the people who were in it. He left none remaining; as he had done to Hebron, so he did to Debir and its king, as he had also done to Libnah and its king.

So Joshua conquered all the land: the mountain country and the South and the lowland and the wilderness slopes, and all their kings; he left none remaining, but utterly destroyed all that breathed, as the LORD God of Israel commanded.

And Joshua conquered them from Kadesh Barnea as far as Gaza, and all the country of Goshen, even as far as Gibeon. All these kings and their land Joshua took at one time, because the LORD God of Israel fought for Israel.

Then Joshua returned, and all Israel with him, to the camp at Gilgal (Josh. 10: 28-43).

Warfare such as this led to the almost total annihilation of the original inhabitants of ancient Palestine, who fell into the hands of Israelites led by Joshua. The only peoples spared, we are informed, were those who were able to trick Israelite leaders into believing that they did not occupy territory being reserved for the worship of the Israelite God, Yahweh. This was the case of the inhabitants of Gibeon, who, when negotiating their surrender, deceived the Israelites into believing that they had come from far away. The Israelites therefore deviated from Yahweh's command and accepted their peaceful submission. However, the Gibeonites were enslaved, becoming "woodcutters and water carriers for all the congregation..." (Josh. 9: 21).

(Excerpts from *The Holy Bible: Containing the Old and NewTestaments*, New King James Version)

The Destruction of the Idolaters and Mass Destruction among Other Ancient People

To an extent, the destruction of the idolaters follows a pattern of conquest and destruction pursued by other ancient groups, with the Israelite tribes being but one of the nomadic groups taking possession of the city-states that had been established around them. In ancient times, conquest in itself gave the conquerors absolute power over the conquered. Initially, the conquerors used this power to sacrifice to their gods any captives taken in war. Such a practice was common, for example, among the early Sumerians and Greeks.[1] A more complete destruction was common among groups related to the Israelites, such as the Moabites. Thus, Mesha, son of KMSH[YT], king of Moab, reports his having taken Nebo from Israel, following which he slew all the inhabitants, consisting of seven thousand men, women and children, for he had consecrated it to Ashtar-Chemosh.[2] Lüdemann adds that the Moabite inscription, dating from the year 830 BC, which is recorded in a language very similar to biblical Hebrew, suggests that the Moabite practice of the ban, or the total destruction of a people so as to satisfy the demands of a deity, may be explained by the common background between the Israelites and the Moabites.[3]

There is little evidence that ancient conquerors other than the Israelites and the Moabites placed such extreme emphasis on the total destruction of peoples they conquered. Thus, conquest was comparatively less destructive among ancient Hittites, who focussed on negotiation rather than brute force to take over a territory. Cities were encouraged to submit willingly, to negotiate conditions under which they would surrender. In these cases, the Hittites concentrated on seeking allies rather than subjugating a population. If a city nevertheless chose to go to war rather than submit, it was destroyed; its territory was dedicated to the thunder god, and its inhabitants dispersed as serfs among Hittite nobles.[4] The Assyrians were at the other extreme. Although a fortified city could negotiate conditions under which it would submit, the Assyrians targeted certain cities that refused to submit, slaughtering most of its inhabitants so as to terrorize future target groups, discouraging them from resisting Assyrian expansion.[5] Mass destruction in this instance, however, was dictated by tactics of war rather than by the desire to meet the demands of a particular deity.

The Greeks also pursued other patterns. For example, Thucydides describes the encounter between the ambitious Athenians and the Malians who resisted them. The Athenian speech to the Malians, in Thucydides' account, gives insight into Athenian motives and actions:

> We on our side will use no fine phrase saying... that we have a right to our empire because we defeated the Persians, or that we have come against you because of the injuries you have done us - a great mass of words that nobody would believe.... You know as well as we do that, when these matters are discussed by practical people, the standard of justice depends on the equality of power to compel and that in fact the strong do what they have the power to do and the weak accept what they have to accept.[6]

According to Thucydides, the Athenians did not press the siege seriously. Due to some treachery inside the city, the Malians surrendered to the Athenians, who put to death the grown men and sold the women and children as slaves. Subsequently, Athens sent out five hundred colonists to inhabit the place.

Writing of Rome, Fustel De Coulanges states that its soldiers made war, not only upon other soldiers, but upon an entire population - men, women, and children. A war might result in the total destruction of a people, and change a fertile country into a desert. It was by virtue of this law of war that the Romans extended an uninhabited cordon around their city: of the territory where the Volscians had twenty-three cities, they created the Pontine marshes; the fifty-three cities of Latium disappeared; in Samnium, the route taken by Roman armies was less recognized by what remained of their camps than by the unpopulated landscape.[7]

An example of the Roman pattern of conquest at its extreme is the destruction of Carthage at the conclusion of the Punic Wars in 146 BC. Prior to the city's destruction, the Romans gave the Carthaginians the choice of resisting, which would be interpreted as a declaration of war, or vacating their city, which the Romans would then destroy. When Carthage refused to surrender, the Romans attacked and conquered the city, killing many of the Carthaginians in the process. Following this, the city was torn down, the territory where it had stood was sown with salt, and its people were sold into slavery.[8]

In some cases, Israelite patterns of conquest were not dissimilar from these examples. This was the case where the conquered did not occupy territory which the Israelites had reserved for the worship of their deity. Thus, we read in Deuteronomy:

> When you go near to a city to fight against it, then proclaim an offer of peace to it. And it shall be that if they accept your offer of peace, and open to you, then all the people who are found in it shall be placed under tribute to you, and serve you. Now if the city will not make peace with you, but makes war against you, then you shall besiege it. And when the LORD your God delivers it into your hands, you shall strike every male in it with the edge of the sword. But the women, the little ones, the livestock, and all that is in the city, you shall plunder for yourself; and you shall eat the enemies' plunder which the LORD your God gives you. Thus you shall do to all the cities which are very far from you, which are not cities of these nations (Deut. 20: 10-15).

This practice stood in contrast to the treatment the Israelites under Joshua meted out to peoples who occupied land reserved for the worship of Yahweh. Here, the conquest was an integral part of the Israelite religion and the relationship the community had with its deity:

> But of the cities of these peoples which the LORD your God gives you as an inheritance, you shall let nothing that breathes remain alive, but you shall utterly destroy them: the Hittite and the Amorite and the Canaanite and the Perizzite and the Hivite and the Jebusite, as the LORD your God has commanded you, lest they teach you to do according to all their abominations which they have done for their gods, and you sin against the LORD your God (Deut. 20: 16-17).

Scripture further justifies this severity by placing the destruction into the larger context of war among ancients, when it states: "For it was the LORD'S doing to harden their hearts that they should come against Israel in battle, in order that they should be utterly destroyed, and should receive no mercy but be exterminated, as the LORD commanded Moses" (Josh. 11:20). At the same time, the Israelite destruction of the idolaters went beyond the manner in which most ancient peoples treated the conquered. It was more extreme because of the nature of the Israelite relationship to their God.

No matter whether it was the Sumerians, the Hittites, the Babylonians, the Assyrians or other ancient conquerors, none was commanded to slaughter all the inhabitants on the territory reserved for the worship of their gods. In fact, the opposite tended to be the case. Conquest often meant adding the stable of deities of the conquered to their deities and thereby being strengthened. It was almost as if these deities were seen to represent energies. By assimilating the deities of the conquered people, the conquerors absorbed the energy represented by these deities, enabling them to solicit their support for their own purposes.

The followers of the Israelite deity, Yahweh, however, did not see themselves strengthened through the acquisition of other deities. Rather, they saw God's anger being raised against His people. The idolaters were destroyed to minimize the possibility of the community's being punished by Yahweh and maximize the possibility of its being rewarded by Him. To further encourage this, God commanded that Israelites themselves who deviated from worshipping the tribal deity and encouraged others to leave the tribal religion be killed. Not only that, He commanded that their cities be destroyed and all therein killed (Deut. 13:1-18). This served to ensure that only one God, the God of Israel, would be worshipped by the Israelites.

With conquerors such as the Babylonians or Romans, on the other hand, a people could be destroyed or become one with the conqueror through the sharing of deities. The account we have in the Book of Joshua is written from an entirely different perspective. The objective of the Israelite invaders, as presented to us from the point of view of the writers, was to totally destroy the followers of other gods, wipe them out, so that the Holy Land could become the territorial base for the Israelite God. The purpose of the slaughter was ultimately to create a place on earth where the believers in Yahweh could practice their religion without the threat of contamination from non-believers. It was carried out to ensure that on this territory the blessings of the tribal deity would flow toward His people and make the land He had chosen for them the next best thing to Paradise.[9]

God, Humankind and the Ideal Existence in the Temporal Sphere

The holocaust and the salvation promised to the people of Israel in the Book of Joshua of the Old Testament illustrate a specific view of the good life, of God and humankind. They present an image of a deity who is seen both as universal and as preferring a specific group of people, namely the offspring of Abraham. However, the Israelites can be assured of His blessings only if they abide by the religious practices and by the laws God prescribed for them. At the same time, if they don't follow the religious practices and instead deviate from the behavior required of them, God threatens not merely to withdraw His favors from them but to destroy them.

The conclusion one can reach from this is that while the God of the Old Testament has chosen to give preference to a certain ethnicity, this preference continues only as long as this ethnic group abides by the rules and the religious practices the tribal deity established as the proper form of worship for Him. This means, ultimately, that belief and behavior are the most important criteria God has for sustaining His relationship with a particular group.

Of course, the idolaters who occupied the Holy Land at the time of the Israelite invasion weren't given that choice. God demanded that these be destroyed so that His chosen could be provided with the best conditions that would enable them to reap the rewards and avoid the punishment of their tribal deity.

This presents essentially two views regarding the value of human life. One view concerns God's relationship with the elect. These are given essentially two choices. If they choose to worship God in a manner He demands of them, they have the possibility of living a life that approximates conditions of Paradise. If they fail to do so, they are threatened with destruction.

The idolaters are depicted essentially as a negative force. As far as God is concerned, they have to be destroyed, so that the people He chose as His beloved are given the best opportunity of gaining His blessings. More than this, God even participates in the battles to ensure that the Israelites would destroy them.

At the same time, the destruction of the idolaters and the establishment of the Holy Land, the view of God, of humankind and the ideal existence in the temporal sphere appear very much influenced by the story of the Garden of Eden, where the first man and woman lived in Paradise. Although on earth, the inhabitants of Paradise suffered neither sickness, war, nor death. God lived among them as long as they abided by the rules He had established for them. This blessed state ended when Adam and Eve deviated from the rules God had set for them.

Thus, there was a close relationship between abiding by the laws of God and Paradise. Furthermore, Paradise was created, not through human effort, but was a reward of faithfulness and obedience. Thus, it is reasonable that the main goal of the Israelites, when seeking to establish for themselves an environment approximating Paradise to the extent that was humanly possible, was to create an environment in which they could best meet the demands of their deity.

In a world dominated by polytheism, where the Israelites were seeking to establish a monotheistic religion, it was natural that they should target other religions as the main threat to their monotheistic faith. Their solution was to destroy the followers of all other religions on the territory where they hoped to be rewarded by their deity with an ideal existence. This existence, while not Paradise, through its promise of safety, fruitfulness, abundance and well being, approximated Paradise to the extent that it was possible in the temporal sphere.

In terms of this conceptualization, the main abode for human beings was earth. This is where people could find Paradise to whatever extent it was possible. This ideal state, however, was not a product of one's doing, but was bestowed by the deity. In the case of the Israelites, it was bestowed upon the community as a whole and, as such, was a reward for carrying out the religious rituals and abiding by the rules their God had established for them.

The idolaters were slaughtered so as to enable the Israelites to best attain the ideal conditions to which they aspired. The slaughter was carried out by the Israelite men of war acting under the direction of their leader, who, in turn, was advised and helped through the active participation of the tribal deity, on whose command the slaughter was carried out. In some respects, the idolaters are of no concern to the God of Israel other than that they do not foil the endeavor by His chosen to gain His blessings. At the same time, they are seen as worthy of absolute destruction because they worship false gods. In the case of both the Israelites and the idolaters, reward and punishment takes place in time and space, as we know it.

As such, the total destruction of one group of people was closely integrated with assuring that another group of people could enjoy the ideal existence to which they aspired. At the same time, the destruction was more than this. It also had a justification in religious terms. All ancient deities required sacrifice, in particular blood sacrifice, in order to win the favor of the gods and avoid their punishment. In Greek religious practice, such sacrifices were generally carried out to satisfy the demands of gods of the upper world and those of the lower world. In the case of sacrifices to gods of the upper world, human beings participated in the sacrifice by consuming part of the sacrifice that was being burned to gain the support of a munificent deity. In the case of gods of the lower world, who were seen to be punitive in nature, the entire sacrifice, the sacrifice identified as a "holocaust," was burned or handed over to the deity to persuade it not to harm the community or individual members thereof. In many respects, the idolaters were victims of this pattern of destruction. They were committed to total destruction so as to satisfy the needs of the punitive aspect of the Israelite deity. Having satisfied these needs, the Israelites were in a better position to gain access to the rewarding part of their God. The destruction, as such, served not only practical purposes but also formed an integral part of the religious rituals through which ancients sought to avoid punishment and win favor with their God or gods.

2
Armageddon and the Creation of the New Jerusalem

As in the case of the destruction of the idolaters, the destruction of non-believers described in the Book of Revelation, the last book of the Bible, also promises a blessed existence to an elect group. In this case, such is promised, not to Israelite tribal society, but to members of the Christian Church, the body of Christ, as well as to Jews who remain true to the faith. At the same time, Revelation seeks to illustrate that there is a continuity between God's promise of salvation for the Israelites and His promise of salvation for the followers of Christ. This is spelled out in a series of visions encountered by John while on the island of Patmos.

The traditional view is that John recorded his visions around 95 to 96 AD, near the end of the reign of the emperor Domitian who persecuted the Christians in an effort to force them to worship him as a god. This was not a problem for people with many gods, who merely had to add the emperor to the gods they already worshipped. However, the Jews looked upon the practice as idolatrous. On the basis of their special status, recognized by the Romans since the days of Julius Caesar, they tended to be exempt from such worship. Like the Jews, Christians also saw emperor worship as a sign of idolatry. However, the exemption was not extended to the Christians. Force, including murder, was used to have them conform.[1]

A more recent interpretation, that of John Marshall, argues that the Book of Revelation was written, not between 95 and 96 AD, but at the time of the Judean War (66 to 70 AD). Coinciding with the last years of reign of the emperor Nero (54-68 AD), it also witnessed the severe persecution of Christians.[2] The Book expresses the concern which John, a Jewish Christian living in Asia Minor, had regarding Roman cultural and religious domination of the Mediterranean world at that time. He saw such influence as having a potentially damaging effect on Jewish religious practices and life. The Book of Revelation, argues Marshall, was intended to apprise John's fellow believers of the true nature of Roman cultural and religious suppression and to warn his co-religionists, be they Christians or Jews, not to succumb to its domination.[3]

Therefore, Marshall sees the Book of Revelation expressing not merely Christian concerns, but also those of practising Jews. No doubt, the promise of Christ's return and with it the collapse of all heathen empires would have offered solace to both Jews and Christians at the time. This would have been true in particular for Jews such as John, who was also a Christian. In this, they would have been encouraged by Christ's saying, "Assuredly, I say to you, there are some standing here who shall not taste death till they see the Son of Man coming in His kingdom" (Matthew 16: 28).

Persecution would no doubt have encouraged people such as John to look forward to this promise, and with it the arrival of the kingdom of God. The main thrust of John's argument is that while Satan and his obstructive work could retard this development; they would be unable to stop it. Christ's followers shouldn't lose faith. It would be a desperate struggle because Satan wouldn't easily give up his grip on the world. That, however, shouldn't discourage believers, but rather encourage them to focus even more assiduously on their preaching and exorcisms. These were part of God's struggle against Satan and would expedite the inevitable coming of the kingdom of God. In the meantime, God's chosen would have to suffer persecutions of the beast, as prophesied by Daniel. They would have to suffer earthquakes, the blotting out of the sun and moon, infestations and diseases of various kinds, as well as other tribulations. All these, ultimately, were little more, however, than the assurance of their final salvation and victory.[4]

While Jesus was alive, His followers were unclear as to whether He was the Messiah who would liberate the Israelites from the Roman yoke, or had been sent by the Almighty to usher in some major cataclysmic event of significance, not only for the people of Israel, but for humanity as a whole. Daniel had already spoken of the "Son of Man," human in form and yet divine, becoming involved in an end-of-time struggle that would usher in the victory of faithful Jews over the heathens. Jesus himself spoke of the "Son of Man" descending from heaven, accompanied by angels,

Armageddon and the Creation of the New Jerusalem

to judge humankind. However, He didn't make clear whether He was the "Son of Man," or whether He was speaking of someone whose arrival He was prophesying.

With Christ's death and the ensuing resurrection, however, His followers became convinced that He was in fact the divine being suggested in the prophetic vision of the "Son of Man." The epistles of Paul speak of Jesus' return, speak of a Final Judgement in which Jesus would act as God's representative to judge all of humankind. The Acts speak of God having set the day on which the world would be judged. God Himself would choose someone to represent Him at that time. The resurrection served as proof for Christ's followers that He in fact would be the one whom God had chosen to bring about the end of the world as we know it, after which would follow the judgement of both the living and the dead.

Christ himself prophesied the coming of the Final Judgment, with Matthew attributing the following to Christ:

> When the Son of Man comes in His glory, and all the holy angels with Him, then He will sit on the throne of His glory. All the nations will be gathered before Him, and He will separate them one from another, as a shepherd divides his sheep from the goats. And He will set the sheep on His right hand, but the goats on the left. Then the King will say to those on His right hand, "Come, you blessed of My Father, inherit the kingdom prepared for you from the foundation of the world: for I was hungry and you gave Me food...." Then He will also say to those on the left hand, "Depart from Me, you cursed, into the everlasting fire prepared for the devil and his angels: for I was hungry and you gave Me no food..." (Matthew 25: 31-46).

As may be observed from the above, Christ saw a person's thoughts and actions rather than tribal membership as the determining factor deciding whether he or she was destined for heaven or hell. This is also suggested when He states: "And I say to you that many will come from east and west, and sit down with Abraham, Isaac, and Jacob in the kingdom of heaven. But the sons of the kingdom will be cast out into outer darkness. There will be weeping and gnashing of teeth" (Matthew 8: 11-12). And then again, "Therefore as the tares are gathered and burned in the fire, so will it be at the end of this age. The Son of Man will send out His angels, and they will gather out of His kingdom all things that offend, and those who practice lawlessness, and will cast them into the furnace of fire. There will be wailing and gnashing of teeth. Then the righteous will shine forth as the sun in the kingdom of their Father" (Matthew 13: 40-43). Thus, choice and behaviour ensuing therefrom were the main criteria Christ saw as determining who would count among the saved, with religious or tribal membership being less important than doing the will of the Lord.

Although Christ's death and crucifixion initially raised some doubt, in particular among some of His followers, His resurrection not merely restored but reinforced their faith in His divinity. At the same time, it caused them to reinterpret the significance of Christ not only for themselves, or for Jews, but also for all of humankind. Christ, the Son of God, would usher in the end of the world, as we know it. He came to make people aware of the final judgment. The Book of Revelation builds on this, presenting a message of hope to believers at a time of tribulation, telling them that although they may have to suffer now, they should retain the faith. After all, their suffering will be temporary. Their reward, once the kingdom of God manifests itself, will be eternal joy and blessedness.

Traditionally, the author of the Book of Revelation was assumed to have been the Apostle John, the son of Zebedee. Therefore, first and second-century Fathers of the Church included Revelation as part of the New Testament canon. However, the Book doesn't suggest apostolic authorship, but rather the work of another Jewish convert to Christianity, who was convinced that Christ fulfilled the promises of the God of Abraham for all true believers, be they Christians or Jews.

Intimately familiar with scripture, John drew heavily on different parts of the Old Testament, such as Zachariah and in particular the Book of Daniel, to present his argument that Christ offered salvation to both Christians and Jews. Thus, his 144,000 "servants of God," with seals upon their foreheads to protect them from the

Armageddon and the Creation of the New Jerusalem 35

catastrophes to be visited upon the rest of humankind, included both non-Jews and members of the twelve tribes of Israel. The reference also suggests an earlier period of Israelite salvation, when God saved the Israelites from the punishments He imposed on the Egyptians for refusing to let His people depart for the Holy Land. Also, the visionary identifies heaven, the abode of eternal blessedness for the followers of Christ and for Jews who remained true to the faith, with Jerusalem. The foundation stones of the city wall have inscribed in them the names of the twelve apostles. Over its twelve gates are inscribed the names of the twelve tribes of Israel. In its resplendent glory, this heavenly Jerusalem, however, is totally free of non-believers, never to be defiled by them, with the saved including both Jews and people from other nations who accepted Christ as their savior.

The Book of Revelation begins with John experiencing a vision of Jesus' day of resurrection. What starts as a vision of the resurrected Jesus, climaxes in a whole series of visions that, in their totality, prophesy the end of time, the destruction of life as we know it, and the creation of a new heaven and a new earth. Expanding on canonical and apocalyptic concepts rooted in Jewish and Christian thought, John applies flashbacks and flash forwards to present his divinely revealed message of how the temporal world will end. His experiences are related through what might be called four movements. The first movement is initiated by a throne scene showing the scroll of judgement, with no one able to open its many seals until the appearance of the Lamb (Lion of Judah, root of David). Although He had been slain, the Lamb is alive. He opens six of the seven seals. As each is opened, a catastrophe leaps forth. The catastrophes are not yet, however, poured unto the earth. Before this is done, a symbolic number of the faithful would be marked with a visible number on their foreheads, which would allow them to escape the coming disasters. This is followed by a vision of the vast throng of those who have endured what is to take place. Following this, the last seal is broken. It is only then that the disasters are loosened, each of them heralded by a trumpet blast. Rather than take these as warnings, calling upon it to repent, humankind continues its rebellion against God. In this situation, two witnesses appear in the temporal Jerusalem. They are killed by the beast from the bottomless pit, but then are resurrected. The last trumpet sounds, announcing the inauguration of the kingdom of the Lord God and His Christ, who shall reign forever and ever.

With this, the second movement commences, returning us to the origin of the Christian Church. Lacking the power to obliterate the newly born Church, which is identified with Jesus, the great dragon makes war on believers. To do so, the dragon calls upon the beast of the sea. Like himself, the beast, which has many crowned heads, has great power. Deceived by him, ordinary people are swayed to worship his power as he persecutes Christians and other adherents of the true faith. Then, a little beast, which resembles a lamb, appears. It creates a seemingly alive image of the beast from the sea. It then uses the threat of death to force people to worship it. Also, to trade or otherwise function successfully in society, one must bear the mark of the beast on one's forehead. Seven angels pour seven bowls of the Lord's wrath onto earth, which cause people to further rebel against God.

The next movement begins, showing all the powers of the world, led by two beasts, gathering at Armageddon to battle against God. There are scenes of great bloodletting in which Jesus, the slain Lamb, battles the forces of the beasts and the horde of humanity allied with them. In these battles, the kingly Jesus emerges victorious. The beast from the sea as well as the false prophet (the lamb-beast) are captured and tossed into the lake of fire. The multitude of people that had allied themselves with the beasts are killed with the sword from Jesus' mouth. The dragon, or Satan, is chained in the bowels of the earth for a thousand years. Christians and Jews who had not deviated from the faith, and had been slain by the beasts, are resurrected to reign with Jesus for a thousand years over the unreconstructed world. At the end of this time, the dragon is freed. Thereupon, he rouses the unredeemed world to do battle against God and Christ. In the wars that ensue, his forces are annihilated by a blast of heavenly fire. He is then tossed into the lake of fire. This is followed by the resurrection of humankind and the final judgement. Following the judgment, the wicked, or all those who had deviated from Judaism or had not accepted Christ as their savior and had not walked in His ways, are sent down to the lake of fire. The redeemed, or those who have been cleansed by the blood of the Lamb (in other words, members of

Armageddon and the Creation of the New Jerusalem

the Christian Church who have remained faithful to Christ and his teachings) and Jews who remained true to the faith enter into eternal bliss, to worship God and the Lamb forever.

The last movement presents a vision of the new heaven and the new earth, to be created after the destruction of the existing heaven and earth. It will be free of all sinners and evildoers, be they Jews fallen away from the faith or Gentiles who had not accepted the Lord Jesus Christ as their savior. These people, together with Satan, will suffer forever in the lake of fire. The redeemed will enjoy the New Jerusalem, the new heaven and earth. Here there will be neither darkness nor suffering. Nor will there be death. Together with the angels, the redeemed will live forever in eternal bliss.

Holy Land and the New Jerusalem: Similarities and Differences

Similarities

The Holy Land and the New Jerusalem share several characteristics and also differ in significant ways. Thus, in both the establishment of the Holy Land and the creation of the new heaven and the new earth, we have a God at work who is perceived as being all-powerful. He created heaven and earth. Although He permits other deities to act upon the world, they act essentially to present people with moral choices.

In both cases the destruction is part of a moral evolution. This, in turn, rests upon several suppositions. One is that for the good to be attained and for the good to sustain itself, evil and all associated with it have to be eradicated. In fact, the two are exclusive. As such, the destructions form part of a moral development, a development based on the belief that a person's worthiness in the eyes of God can finally only be attained through the destruction of that which God identifies as evil. In all this, God is seen as being fair and just. People are by nature wicked. It is only God's mercy that keeps Him from utterly destroying humankind. Wickedness and those who follow it are worthy, finally, not only of destruction but also of eternal punishment, just as those who act and believe rightly are worthy, finally, of salvation and eternal blessedness. To ultimately attain their salvation, the wicked have to be eliminated. In many respects, their destruction becomes indelibly linked to establishing the ideal environment for the elect groups.

Differences

In the one case, the ideal environment was created in time and space. It had a territorial dimension. In the other case, the ideal locale is a new world, a new heaven and a new earth. These would be created after life on earth, as we know it, has been destroyed, essentially because of man's wickedness. In the one case, in the establishment of the Holy Land, people are killed to create an ideal environment for the Lord's chosen. In the case of Armageddon, evildoers are not necessarily killed but rather are sent down to hell where, together with Satan, they will be punished forever. Except for the pain suggested by the images of the fires of hell, what is being described here is beyond the ken of our experiences.

There is a change in the manner in which utopia is attained. In the case of the establishment of the Holy Land, Israelite tribes draw on faith in God and depend on God's help to create an environment in which they can be assured of God's blessings. Both man and God act in conjunction in an attempt to establish a place of worship on earth where the elect would not be polluted by the belief systems of other peoples. In this process, God acts as advisor. At the same time, He participates in the destruction of nonbelievers so as to create an environment for the Israelites that will be the next best thing to Paradise.

In the Book of Revelation, battles are also fought to bring about an idealized state of existence. However, they are not so much fought by people as by God through Christ, the slain Lamb, the Son of God, who battles his main opponent, the Antichrist and the host that supports him, to bring about the universal triumph of good over evil and the salvation of all true believers, both Jewish and Christian. In this case, belief is identified with righteousness and disbelief is ultimately an expression of wickedness, it being naturally assumed that wickedness ensues from non-belief. The battles fought have little to do with reality, as we know it, but are in many ways mythological in nature. The same is true of the eternal blessedness being promised.

Armageddon and the Creation of the New Jerusalem

In the case of the Holy Land, God essentially chooses who is worthy of salvation. Thus we read: "You are the children of the Lord your God; you shall not cut yourselves or shave the front of your head for the dead. For you are a holy people to the Lord your God, and the Lord has chosen you for Himself, a special treasure above all the peoples who are on the face of the earth" (Deut. 14: 1-2).

The situation is quite different in the case of the Book of Revelation. Sonship and holiness are not bestowed upon a tribal community. Rather, the idea of sonship and holiness is concentrated in Christ, who is seen as both human and divine. Salvation is not granted essentially on the basis of ethnic membership. Rather, the individual can choose whether he wishes to belong among the redeemed or among the damned. For the Jew, the choice is whether he wishes to follow Jewish religious practices or choose Christ as his savior. For the Gentile, the choice is choosing Christ as his savior or eternal perdition.

Thus, in summary:

-One destruction is earth-centred and in time as we know it;
-the other is part of a larger cosmic battle at the end of time.
-The Holy Land is established to provide the conditions where a tribal society can best serve its deity;
-Christians and Jews who remain true to the faith enter heaven where they are free to worship Christ and God without the interference of non-believers.
-In establishing the Holy Land, God and man act together;
-in the Book of Revelation, God acts through the slain Lamb to destroy evil and create the new heaven and earth.
-When the Holy Land is established, battles take place against specific, identifiable groups;
-in the Book of Revelation, battles are fought against vaguely defined forces of evil.
-In the one case, the elect of God are promised the Holy Land where, in return for serving their deity, they will find themselves in a situation in this life that is the next best thing to Paradise;
-in the other case, Jews who had remained true to the faith and people who have accepted Jesus Christ as their savior and have remained loyal in serving him, are promised a new heaven

and earth where they will exist in eternal bliss. In this situation, the choice was made in life and the rewards are in the afterlife.

Getting from the Holy Land to the New Jerusalem

The question may well be asked: what is it in the biblical account that results in salvation being offered in the temporal sphere in the one case and at some vague end-of-time future in the other? What might one look at in the Bible to isolate the dynamics that contributed to this progression? Do some elements of the belief system under discussion remain constant? Do some elements change, and in what respects do they change so as to lead to a particular conclusion? What might one look at to determine what remained constant and what changed?

There are certain elements in the biblical account as well in Israelite history one might look at to answer these questions. Some of these are fairly obvious, and others less so. Nevertheless, exploring these elements helps to illustrate the pattern of evolution that leads to a paradise-like existence being promised in the temporal sphere at the beginning of the Bible to eternal bliss in heaven being promised in the afterlife at its conclusion. Evidence of this progression may be observed in the Israelite historical experience, as becomes evident when one looks at the evolution of Israelite history as suggested in the Bible and other sources. It is also illustrated by the manner in which this historical experience was used to perpetuate the faith by those who prepared the biblical account.

In particular, certain key elements in the historical record and the interpretation thereof give insight into the evolution. In this regard, the view of humanity and God, and the relationship between God and His chosen are of special significance. This relationship is structured in particular by God's use of reward and punishment to educate His chosen. Thus, the evolution from rewards promised in the Holy Land to those promised in the New Jerusalem have very much to do with the manner in which God rewards His elect. Perhaps even more important, the evolution is structured by the manner in which God punished in particular the people of Israel when they failed to follow Him.

Armageddon and the Creation of the New Jerusalem

Furthermore, the progression from the Holy Land to the New Jerusalem is also reflected in the role that the savior, or what eventually came to be known as the messiah, played in Israelite history. Thus, I will look at the evolution of the view of the messiah as he is presented in Scripture. I will examine his role in helping his community out of a difficult situation, his role as the Son of Man described in the Book of Daniel, as Christ the Messiah and then as the slain Lamb who battles the forces of evil in the Book of Revelation.

In summary, the study will look at the biblical record, at the historical experience of the Israelites as depicted in this record and other sources, at different ideas developed in the Bible regarding God, humankind, and the relationship between them, so as to illustrate the evolution that led from salvation and the ideal existence being offered in the temporal sphere at the beginning of the Bible and in the eternal sphere at its end. At the same time, it will seek to show how salvation and the ideal existence for one group in each case was an integral part of the elimination of another group, be this through being killed or being expelled to hell and perdition.

Part II

Events and the Record Thereof

3
A Chronology of Israelite History

The following provides a brief chronological overview of the Israelite historical experience as presented in the Bible, dating from the time when Israel was first established to the time when the Book of Revelation was apparently written, when the Jews were under Roman rule. While the dates are taken from a variety of historical sources, the events are mirrored in the Bible. As such, the term "Israel" refers to the Hebrew people. First united as a tribal confederacy, they became one nation under David. The nation split into two, Judah and Israel, after the death of Solomon. These competed with each other until the Assyrians conquered Israel and expelled its inhabitants. Judah, which survived, gave its name to its inhabitants, the Jews, who persisted as a single people and continue to this day.

1200-1020 BC
The conquest of Canaan by the Israelites and the destruction of the idolaters, followed by Israel's being ruled by Judges, who were essentially religious leaders.

1020-965
The establishment of monarchical rule under Saul, followed by the establishment of the united monarchy under David.

965-928
The Reign of Solomon, the golden age of Israel, during which the Temple was built in Jerusalem.

928-721
Following the death of Solomon, the division of the united monarchy into two kingdoms, Israel and Judah. These competed

with each other to the point where they invited other powers to side with them in their quarrels. This weakened both kingdoms, accelerating their decline and their conquest by other powers.

721
Assyria conquered the northern kingdom, Israel, and expelled its inhabitants. Judah continued as an Assyrian vassal.

597
First deportation of Judah's elites by Babylon, which, after its conquest of Assyria, became the major empire in the region.

587
Nebuchadnezzar of Babylon destroys Jerusalem, following the revolt by his vassal, King Zedekiah. Nebuchadnezzar deports many of Judah's leading citizens to Babylon.

582
The third deportation of inhabitants of Judah by the Babylonians, supplemented by refugees from Egypt.

587-538
Nebuchadnezzar's family is ousted from power in Babylon. Nabonidus is crowned king. He alienates many Babylonians by fostering the worship of Sin, the moon-god, at the expense of the national deity, Marduk. This weakens Babylon against the rising power of Persia.

538-537
The Persians, under Cyrus II (c.550-529 BC), conquer Babylon. Rather than expel conquered populations, Cyrus encourages people who had been conquered by the Babylonians to return to their homelands. At the same time, he also returned to their former homes gods that had been taken captive by the Babylonians as they conquered other peoples. In the case of the Israelites, who didn't have an image of their deity, he returned the utensils of the House of God to Jerusalem.

Cyrus believed this would earn him the gratefulness as well as the support of local deities. Therefore he encouraged local religions. In the case of Israel, this encouraged a separation of church and state, with the state being dominated by a foreign power and the religion dominated by Judah's priesthood.

522
With the encouragement of the Persians, Zerubbabel leads a second party of Jews from Babylon to Jerusalem and begins to build the Second Temple.

445
Nehemiah establishes Jerusalem as a Persian administrative unit.

330-327
Alexander of Macedonia completes the conquest of Persia. With this, Greece replaces Persia as the dominant power in Palestine.

323
Alexander dies after establishing an empire over most of the known world. Following this, Palestine passes to the Ptolomies, then to the Seleucids, both Macedonian Greek rulers.

323-285
Ptolemy (I) Soter rules in Egypt.

300
Palestine passes to Ptolemaic control. During this time, many Jews emigrate or are transported to Alexandria.

246-203
Rule of Ptolemies III and IV. During this time, the Suptuagint, a Greek-language version of Hebrew scripture, appears. The translation is completed ca. 150, in Alexandria.

200-198
Palestine, conquered by Antiochus III (223-187), falls under the rule of Seleucid Greeks of Syria.

198
Rome begins to interfere with Greek rule in Palestine, which results in the defeat of Seleucid Greeks at Magnesia.

175-163
Antiochus IV Ephiphanes rules Judah. He discards the traditional Greek policy of tolerance in religious matters and seeks to impose emperor worship on the Jews.

168-167
The Temple in Jerusalem is desecrated by Hellenizers and Seleucids.

168-164
Antiochus IV attempts to suppress the Jewish religion and the Jewish way of life.

166
A revolt, led by Judas (166-160), erupts against the Seleucids and the Jewish Hellenizers.

164-160
To strengthen its position against the Greeks, Judah, or Judea as it came to be known under Greek and Roman rule, renews its alliance with Rome and also pursues an alliance with Sparta. The Temple in Jerusalem is rededicated. The Book of Daniel appears.

142-134
Judea wins complete independence, with the support of Rome. At the same time, supreme religious, military, and civil authority is made hereditary in the Hasmonean family.

134-104
Judea annexes Galilee and Idumaea, and uses force to Judaize the inhabitants. The period also witnesses the proliferation of numerous parties in Judaism.

104-103
Aristobulus I rules Judea.

A Chronology of Israelite History

103-76
Alexander Jannaeus antagonizes the Pharisees by marrying Salome, the widow of his older brother, Aristobulus I. Revolts erupt against him, during which the Pharisees appeal to the Romans for help.

76-67
Assisted by leading Pharisees, Salome rules Judea.

67
Hyrcanus, who prior to this served as high priest, briefly rules as king of Judea. He is ousted by his younger brother, Aristobulus II.

67-63
Civil war erupts between the factions supporting Aristobulus II and those supporting Hyrcanus.

65
Both sides appeal for help to the Romans, who are occupying Syria.

63
After two years of mediation between the Jewish factions, the Romans occupy Jerusalem.

40
The Roman Senate appoints Herod (the Great) king of Judea.

37 BC
Herod conquers Galilee and Judea, and takes office in Jerusalem as "confederate king."

30 AD
Jesus is tried and crucified in about AD 30, bringing to an end his life as teacher.

66-70
Civil war, which includes the struggle against Roman rule and the persecution of Christians, erupts in Palestine.

70

The Romans raze the Temple in Jerusalem.

95-96

The emperor Domitian, expanding upon the "pro forma" divination of emperors, demands that he be acknowledged as a god, and that sacrifices be offered to him.

135

The Romans crush two revolts against their rule. Following the final uprising, in AD 135, most Jews are expelled from Palestine, ending Israel's existence as a political entity.

249-311

The period witnesses short spans of toleration and also endeavours to destroy the Christian Church. These include attempts by the emperors Decius and Valerian to eradicate the Church. This is followed by a "long peace," instituted by Gallienus. In 303, Diocletian and Galerius embark on a policy of cruel suppression. From 305, when Diocletian abdicates, Galerius adds thousands to the martyrs. In 311, the dying persecutor admits defeat and asks Christians to pray for him. In 313 AD, returning victorious from Britain and Gaul, Constantine acknowledges the sovereignty of the Christian God and gives the Christian Church preferential treatment.

From this survey, it becomes evident that following the original conquest, the Jewish people constituted a powerful regional force in Palestine essentially only during the period of the united monarchy, under David and Solomon. It was during these two generations that Israel was at the height of its glory. For most of its history, it was a relatively weak state dominated by other states in the area or under the control of the empires that dominated the Near Middle East, the Assyrian, the Babylonian, the Persian, the Greek, and the Roman. At the same time, the Israelites felt themselves to have the most powerful of deities and the only true god. As ancient peoples believed the destiny of humankind and of nations to be determined by the power of their particular deity or deities, this necessitated that the Israelite priesthood, the priesthood of Yahweh, explain away any defeats that the Israelites suffered in which other peoples came to dominate them. The evolution from the Holy Land to the Book of Revelation very much grew out of the Israelite priesthood's attempt to explain how and why, with the most powerful deity, they nevertheless had to suffer defeats at the hands of their enemies. How this was done may be observed from how they described particularly significant defeats.

4
Recording Historical Events

The historical evolution of Israel, which witnessed a rise in power, a brief domination of the area that came to be known as the Holy Land and then a decline and a long period of subjugation, gave structure to the biblical record. As important, and even more important, perhaps, than the actual history in shaping the evolution of thoughts and ideas we find in the Bible, is the attempt by recorders of the Israelite experience to explain this experience in the light of Israel's relationship to its deity, Yahweh. The Israelites believed that their God was the most powerful and in many ways the only genuine deity active on earth. Nothing was impossible for Him. He was the master over victory as well as defeat. He was certainly powerful enough to grant the Israelites victory over other peoples who came into conflict with them. Much of the biblical historical record, therefore, deals with the attempt to explain why the God Yahweh, the most powerful deity on earth and in heaven, did not grant the Israelites victory over their enemies and made them a subject people for most of their history.

To gain insight into the manner in which the Israelites recorded their history, it may be best to choose a time period for which we have both non-Israelite and Israelite sources. We have very few accounts from the earlier period of Israelite history that would allow us to compare their accounts with those of other peoples. This is not the case once Israel was absorbed into the different world empires that dominated that part of the world in ancient times. One of the earliest records we have in which Israel is mentioned by other people dates back to the Assyrian period. We also have accounts left to us by the Babylonians that relate to the conquest of Jerusalem and the expulsion of the Judahites to Babylon. We have Persian accounts relating to the return of the expelled Judahites to their homes after the Persians conquered Babylon. To gain insight into the manner in which the Israelites recorded history, it would be of interest to compare a sample of the record of these events as found in accounts based on Assyrian, Babylonian or Persian sources with the biblical account left to us, for example, in the Book of Isaiah.

The following summary, dealing with the circumstances that led to the decline of Israel and its absorption into the dominant empires of the Near Middle East was drawn, in part from the biblical record, but primarily from Roux's account, which deals with the subject but is based essentially on non-biblical sources.

The Israelites attained the height of their power under David and Solomon when Israel and Judah were united under a common crown. This union ended with Solomon's death. In part, the problem was caused by the heavy expenditures of Solomon's court and the tax burden this imposed upon the people. As a consequence, Israel chose its own ruler while Solomon's son, Rohoboam, continued to rule Judah. This initiated a prolonged decline of Israelite power, which was caused by several factors, including the outbreak of war between Israel and Judah. The two not only fought each other but also sought to involve other nations in their conflicts. Thus, Asa, King of Judah, entered into an alliance with Syria against Israel, as a result of which Ben-Hadad of Syria sent his armies against Israel and conquered Ijon, Dan, Abel Beth Macha, and all Chinneroth, with all the land of Naphtali (1 Kings 15: 16-21). Simultaneously, dynastic interests took precedence over national interests, which at times resulted in an army general taking over from a king, killing him and his offspring and then placing himself on the throne. Thus, Baasha killed Jeroboam, King of Israel, as well as his entire house, and set himself on the throne (1 Kings 15: 27-30). Zimri, commander of half the king's chariots, in turn, killed Baasha and all his offspring, so that he could take the throne (1 Kings 16: 8-14). Social unrest resulted from monarchs transgressing societal traditions and using their power to enrich themselves. This happened, for example, in the case of King Ahab of Israel and his wife Jezebel, who had the king's neighbour, Noboth, killed so that they could take over his vineyard (1 Kings 21: 1-20). At the same time, disunity arose in the nation as a result of the many deities brought into Israel by the wives of the different kings. This disunity was further encouraged by the Yahwist priesthood itself, with the priests in Jerusalem emphasizing that Jerusalem, in Judah, should be the centre of worship for Yahweh while other groups set up their own centres of worship, resulting in rivalries among the different religious centres.

The incessant warfare with neighbours as well as the invasion of outside peoples seeking to establish themselves in Palestine, and conflict between Israel and Judah, greatly weakened the Hebrews and made them vulnerable to expanding imperial conquerors. The first major conquerors in this regard were the Assyrians. They made several efforts to subjugate lands bordering the Mediterranean, including Israel. Thus, in 853 BC, the Assyrian leader Shalmaneser entered the plains of central Syria with the objective of conquering the territory. He was opposed by Irhuleni of Hama and Adad-idri of Damascus (Ben-Hadad II of the Bible), who led contingents provided by "twelve kings of the sea-coast." Although the Assyrians slew many warriors in these encounters, they took neither Hama nor Damascus. During the next eight years, further expeditions were mounted against Hama with a similar limited success. Still, while the main cities were not captured, numerous towns and villages were looted and burned. In 841 BC, Damascus, then ruled by Hazael, was again attacked. Although his forces were defeated on Mount Sanir (Hermon), Hazael escaped to his capital city. To satisfy his frustration, Shalmaneser could do little more than ravage the gardens surrounding Damascus and plunder the rich plain of Hauran. Following this, he moved on to the coast. On Mount Carmel, he received the tribute of Tyre, Sidon and Iaua mâr Humri (Jehu, son of Omri), King of Israel, the first biblical personage to be mentioned in cuneiform inscription.[1] In 734 BC the Assyrian ruler Tiglathpileser returned to the Mediterranean, where Tyre and Sidon were in turmoil because of Assyrian restrictions on timber exports to Philistia and Egypt. Worse still, the Philistine rulers of Ascalon and Gaza had organized an anti-Assyrian coalition consisting of all the kingdoms of Palestine and Trans-Jordana. Tiglathpileser crushed the rebels. The "man of Gaza" fled to Egypt and the Prina of Ascalon was killed. Amon, Edom, Moab and Judah were forced to pay tribute. Two years later, King Ahaz of Judah, under attack from Damascus and Israel, appealed to the Assyrians for help. Tiglathpileser subjugated Damascus, annexed half of Israel and set up Hoshea as king of Samaria.[2]

During the reign of Tiglathpileser's son, Shalmaneser V (726-722 BC), the puppet king of Israel, Hoshea, rebelled. To defeat him, Shalmaneser besieged Samaria for three years. It is uncertain whether it was he or the next king of Assyria who captured the city.[3] It was at this time that many Israelites were deported.

The deportation of captives was initiated by the Assyrian ruler Tiglathpileser II (774-727 BC). He used it to prevent revolt through undermining the loyalty to local gods and traditions and mixing together the populations of the empire. To forward this, people were forced to vacate entire towns and districts and re-settle in distant regions. They were replaced by people brought in from other areas.[4]

The Babylonians replaced the Assyrians as the major power in the Near East, Assyria's decline being brought on through new invaders, such as the Scythians. At the same time, the empire erupted in civil war, with different princes vying for control. Weakened internally, Assyria eventually lost control over its satellite states. Thus, in the west, Phoenician cities severed their connections with Nineveh. Assyrian control over Palestine became so ineffective that King Josiah of Judah succeeded in promoting his religious reform in Samaria, the former kingdom of Israel.[5] The Babylonians, however, presented the most serious threat for the Assyrians. Taking advantage of Assyria's troubles, they recommenced their traditional struggle for independence. Nabû-apla-usur (Nabopolassar), who belonged to the Kaldû tribe, became the leader of the Babylonian insurrection following the death of Ashurbanipal/Kandalanu, the governor of the Sea-Land. After a year of guerrilla warfare, the Assyrian troops stationed in Nippur were unable to defeat him. On 23 November 626 BC, he occupied the throne of Babylon, and laid the base for what came to be generally known as the 'Chaldean' or 'Neo-Babylonian' kingdom.[6]

From 626 - 614 BC, the conflict between the Babylonians and Assyrians concentrated on taking possession of Assyrian fortified cities in southern Iraq. After a continuous series of attacks and counterattacks, Nabopolassar took Nippur and liberated the whole of Sumer and Akkad. To gain the support of the Elamites, who had recovered their freedom, he returned to them the statues of their gods held captive in Babylon. However, he failed to obtain their military support. He didn't dare launch a full-scale offensive against the Assyrians on his own. His Assyrian rival, Sin-shar-ishkun, who had his authority challenged within his own country, in the meantime sought an alliance with the Egyptians to strengthen his own position within Assyria and against the Babylonians.

This situation was altered when the Medes entered into the fray. Toward the end of 615 BC they invaded Assyria and took Arrapha. The following winter they set out to take Nineveh. Instead of attacking it, they marched south to fall on Assur. After capturing it (614 BC), they inflicted a terrible massacre upon the greater part of the population, plundered the city, and carried off prisoners.[7] Although the Babylonians arrived too late to participate in the battle, Nabopolassar met Cyaxares, the Mede ruler, below the walls of Assur and they "established mutual friendship and peace." Not long after, the alliance was cemented through the marriage of Nabopolassar's son, Nebuchadnezzar, with Cyaxares's daughter, Amytis. From then on, Babylonians and Medes fought hand in hand. Despite this powerful opposition, the Assyrians fought bravely, and Nabopolassar made little headway against them in campaigns along the Euphrates. It was not until the summer of 612 BC that the final assault was launched against Nineveh, Assyria's most important city. Following a two-month siege, the city was captured. The Assyrian king was killed. The great spoil of the city and temple was carried off and the city was turned into a ruin-mound and heaps of debris.[8] This essentially brought to an end Assyrian rule.

When explaining the reasons for the conquest, the Assyrians attributed it to sin.[9] This shows that deviation from ritual practices and transgressions against a deity were used not only by the Israelites but also by other ancients to explain why a deity did not come to their aid. Such an explanation was, of course, natural, as it was God or the gods who were seen to be in control not only of humankind but also of the affairs of the universe, thereby determining the fate not only of the universe but also of mankind in war.

Because the Medes didn't lay claim to the kingdom they had helped to overthrow, the Babylonians controlled Assyria.

However, they neither occupied it nor repaired the damage they had inflicted. Rather, they concentrated on reviving the religious and cultural life of southern Mesopotamia. In their foreign policy, they focussed on protecting their frontiers and on subjugating Syria-Palestine. Having been freed from its Assyrian masters, Syria-Palestine had come under Egyptian control after Pharaoh Necho II invaded it in 609 BC. After defeating and killing King Josiah of Judah, who foolishly sought to block the Egyptian advance, Egyptian troops overran Karkemish and took control of the crossing of the Euphrates. As almost all their trade was with the West and the control of the Phoenician coast and hinterland were even more important to the Babylonians than they had been to the Assyrians, Babylon could little afford to have Egypt control these areas. Nor could it afford to have its gateway to the Mediterranean blocked by the Egyptians.[10]

Getting on in age, Nabopolassar, who had defeated the Assyrians, became increasingly dependent on his son to conduct military operations. In 607 BC crown prince Nabûkudirri-usur (Nebuchadnezzar) was assigned to push the Egyptians out of Syria. Failing for two years to establish bridgeheads at important areas of the Euphrates valley, Nebuchadnezzar launched an attack on Karkemish in May and June 605 BC. Supported by Greek mercenaries, the Egyptian garrison put up a valiant defence, but was eventually defeated and massacred. Babylonian troops then pursued the remainder of the Egyptian army. After being overtaken and defeated, the Egyptians were massacred, which left all of Syria-Palestine open to the Babylonians. They had reached Pelusium, on the Egyptian frontier, when Nebuchadnezzar was informed of his father's death. He immediately returned to Babylon, to be crowned upon his arrival in the capital city (23 Sept. 605 BC).

Although invading Syria had been relatively easy, maintaining control of it proved more difficult. While northern Syrians would show themselves to be submissive on the whole, the Philistines, Phoenicians and Jews didn't graciously accept paying the tribute to Babylon that they had but recently stopped paying to Nineveh. Nor would Egypt willingly abandon its dream of a Syrian "colony." A year after the battle of Karkemish, Nebuchadnezzar was again in Syria, displaying his strength so as to collect tribute from Damascus, Tyre, Sidon and Jerusalem. At the same time, he devastated Ascalon, whose ruler had revolted. In 601 BC, he was involved in a major confrontation with Egypt. In the winter of 598/97 BC, King Jehoiakem of Judah refused to pay tribute. Babylon retaliated and on 16 March 597 BC captured Jerusalem. Jehoiakem was replaced by Zedekiah and 3,000 Hebrews were deported to Babylon. Perhaps the proximity of an Egyptian army and the mistaken belief that he could depend on its support encouraged Zedekiah to revolt. Babylon responded, laying siege to Jerusalem. After eighteen months, the city surrendered (587 BC). Zedekiah was captured while fleeing toward Jericho. The king as well as thousands of Jews were deported, while others fled to Egypt. Jerusalem was plundered, its walls demolished, and the House of the Lord that Solomon had built was burned down.

While the Babylonians were pacifying Judah and Syria, which included a thirteen-year siege of Tyre and the replacement of its king by another, the Medes were progressing in a north-westerly direction, invading Armenia and Cappadocia. Following Nebuchadnezzar's death, Babylonia was thrown into turmoil. After a two-year rule (561-560 BC), his son Awêl-Marduk was replaced by a commoner, a Babylonian general who had married one of Nebuchadnezzar's daughters, Neriglissar. He was succeeded by his son, Labâshi-Marduk, a child, who was murdered after reigning for only two months. In June 556 BC, the Babylonians crowned a high official of Aramaen origin, Nabonidus, as their king. This contributed to further turmoil when Nabonidus encouraged the worship of the moon-god, Sin, at the expense of the national deity, Marduk.

This made the Babylonians easy prey for the Persians under Cyrus II. Cyrus II ascended the Persian throne in 559 B.C., three years prior to the crowning of Nabonidus. The Persians, like the Medes to whom they were closely related, had entered Iran at the end of the second millennium. Advancing gradually across the Iranian plateau, they eventually took control of the mountain range still known as Fars, along the Persian Gulf.[11] At the close of the seventh century BC, they were divided into two kingdoms. Persia proper (between Isfahan and Shiraz) was ruled by the Ariaramnes family, while the country of Anshan (or Anzan), bordering Elam, was ruled by the family of Ariaramnes's brother, Cyrus I. Both kingdoms were Mede vassals. The House of Ariaramnes dominated the House of Cyrus until Cyrus's son, Cambyses I (c. 600-559 BC), married the daughter of Astyages, his Median overlord. Cyrus II was the product of this marriage. At the outset of Nabonidus's reign, Cyrus II paid tribute to his grandfather while ruling a large but isolated district of Iran. In the meantime, he subjugated the Iranian tribes of his neighbourhood.

He was gradually expanding his kingdom, when the Babylonian king, Nabonidus, provided him with the opportunity of gaining an empire. Nabonidus insisted on rebuilding the temple of Sin in Harran, which was then held by the Medes, against whom Nabonidus felt himself powerless. Considering the Persians to be the successors of the Elamites, with whom the Babylonians had frequently co-operated in the past, he requested Cyrus's help, and Cyrus accepted. Hearing of the plot, Astyages demanded that he withdraw from his commitment. When Cyrus refused, war broke out, which resulted in a Persian victory, and gave Cyrus control of both the Persian and the Median kingdoms (550 BC).[12]

On conquering the Medes, Cyrus continued his military expansion and, after some ten years, controlled an empire larger than anything the world had previously witnessed. Lydia, ruled by the fabulously rich Croesus, fell to him (547 BC). The Greek city-states of Iona were subdued one after the other and all of Asian Minor was subjected to Persian rule. Then, Parthia and Aria, kingdoms in eastern Iran, Sogdia and Bactria in Turkestan and Afghanistan, as well as a part of India, came under his rule, with the Persian Empire now stretching from the Aegean to the Pamirs, a distance of almost three thousand miles. Babylon found itself dwarfed by this giant.

Rather than frighten people into obedience, Cyrus sought to win the good will of his new subjects by posing as liberator and treating his prisoners with mercy. At the same time, he respected and even encouraged local cults and customs. This made him popular throughout the Near East. In Babylon, some welcomed the idea of a good prince ruling over them, encouraging the rise of a pro-Persian party, which opposed the rule of Nabonidus and his son Balshazzar. When Cyrus launched his attack against Babylon in the autumn of 539 BC, he was aided not only by the numerical superiority of his army but also by the Babylonian monarch's betrayal by his own people. In the first encounter with the Persians,

Babylonian troops were defeated. In early October, Cyrus again engaged the Babylonians, this time at Opis, on the Tigris. When his own people revolted, Nabonidus massacred them. However, after the battle had raged for about two weeks, the Babylonians were defeated and Nabonidus fled.

When on October 13, 539 BC, Cyrus's troops entered Babylon without battle; large branches were laid out before him.[13] The state of "peace" was imposed on the city. Rather than destroying Babylon, as its rival Nineveh had been destroyed, from the first day of occupation the Persians made every effort to respect Babylonian laws and traditions. Cyrus claimed himself to be the successor of Babylon's national rulers, asserting that he rejoiced in worshipping the Babylonian national god, Marduk.[14]

Of course, the Babylonians were not the only people who were positively affected by Cyrus's policies. Cyrus allowed the different peoples, including the Jews, who had been conquered by the Babylonians and taken captive to Babylon, to return to their homes. At the same time, Cyrus returned to their chapels, the "places that make them happy," the gods of Sumer and Akkad, whom Nabonidus had captured during the war and taken to Babylon. Even the gods of Assyria, that had been taken captive by the Medes, were returned to their temples, which were rebuilt.[15] Cyrus returned the gods of Elam and had their ruined temples rebuilt. As the Jews employed no images of their deity, temple utensils representing the exiled divinity that had been looted by Nebuchadnezzar were returned to Jerusalem. At the same time, Cyrus ordered that the house of God in Jerusalem be rebuilt.[16]

Ultimately, Cyrus had a practical objective in returning these deities to their temples. Commenting on his restoration of all captive gods, he ended with this pious hope:

> May all the gods, whom I have brought into their cities, pray daily before Bel and Nabu for long life for me, and may they speak a gracious word for me and say to Marduk my lord: "May Cyrus, the king who worships you, and Cambyses, his son, be blessed."[17]

Thus, Cyrus saw the gods as forces to the good. Insofar as there was a hierarchy among the gods, the most powerful of them was Marduk. Of course, at that time he was praying to Marduk, the main divinity of the Babylonians.

Interpretation of the most significant of these events for the Jews, namely the destruction of Jerusalem by the Babylonians, the expulsion of Judah's leading citizens, and their return under Cyrus II of Persia, as presented in the Book of Isaiah.

The previous account, based primarily on Assyrian, Babylonian and Persian sources, serves to illustrate the context in which the conquest of Israel and Judah occurred, and to provide insight into the conditions that led to the return of a small remnant of Jews from Babylon. It also suggests that, for most Middle Eastern empires, the Israelites were seen as a relatively insignificant group. There is no indication that other peoples had any special regard for the Israelite God. In fact, for them He was probably less important than the god or gods of more powerful groups, essentially because as a god of a weaker people He didn't receive the same respect as did the gods of stronger communities. Therefore, the account based largely on non-biblical sources differs significantly from accounts left to us in the Bible.

For the Assyrians or the Babylonians, their actions in Israel or Judah were merely part of a pattern of conquest involving the expansion of their empires and the consolidation of their rule over subject peoples. For the Yahwist leadership represented by the prophets, the events, however, in particular the destruction of Jerusalem and of the Temple, were earth shattering. The Jews saw themselves as having the most powerful of gods. He was seen to be above all other gods. Gods rather than men were seen to control the affairs of mankind. This was true not only for Jewish but also for other ancient peoples. For Jews, this raised the question: how was it possible that they, having the support of the most powerful of deities, were not only defeated, but that Jerusalem, their centre of worship, was devastated? Not only that, the Temple, which had been built to serve Yahweh, was destroyed. Judah's most important families were expelled to Babylon. But following this, the expellees and their offspring in Babylon had been allowed to return. Why did this happen? How was all this possible? The Jewish leadership responded at various levels, as may be observed by looking at different biblical accounts, be this in the Book of Isaiah, Jeremiah or Ezekiel, that concern themselves largely with this subject. I will look at the reasons for these destructions presented in the Book of Isaiah, to illustrate the arguments used to justify Yahweh's having allowed in particular the destruction of Jerusalem under Nebuchadnezzar and the return of the small remnant under Cyrus of Persia.

When recording these events, the writer gives the impression that the God of Israel, Yahweh, had directed them. While this is difficult to dispute, it does very much appear that the conquerors were not aware of this. At the same time, the Book of Isaiah mentions events, such as the expulsion of the Egyptians or the destruction of certain cities, which are not supported by the evidence from other sources. Of course, this may have been simply as a result of misinformation. The writer certainly was correct in his description of events regarding the conquest of Judah, the destruction of Jerusalem and the expulsion of its leading inhabitants. This does not lead him to question the power of the God of the Israelites. Rather, he blames the destruction on the sins of the Jewish people. At the same time, he reminds them of their special covenant with their God. Thus, the Book of Isaiah focuses on the following:

a) Justification through sin

This is the most prevalent reason given for the destruction of Jerusalem and the expulsion. At different times different prophets emphasize different types of sins that the people of Israel committed so as to justify the expulsion. Sin ties into the theme of reward and punishment that dominates God's relationship with man as well as the relationship between God and His chosen, the Israelites. Thus, the Book of Isaiah dwells extensively on the different sins committed by the people of Judah to explain why God had allowed the Babylonians to conquer and expel them, and destroy the Lord's temple in Jerusalem. Thus, Isaiah sees the Jewish people having committed all the sins condemned by the Ten Commandments, including worshipping and sacrificing to foreign idols rather than to the true God, Yahweh. They also committed a multitude of other sins, including suppressing the poor and cheating them out of their rightful heritage, as well as selling their brethren into slavery. At the same time, the people were punished because their sinful thoughts and actions had displeased the Lord.

Interconnected with the idea of sin was the idea that the different conquerors were agents of Yahweh. Thus, Nebuchadnezzar was seen as having been sent by God to punish the Israelites for their iniquities. Cyrus, on the other hand, was seen as having been used by God when he allowed the Jews in Babylon to return to their homeland. One exiled the people of Judah to punish them and the other permitted them to return to give them another opportunity to gain glory through their loyalty to Yahweh.

Connected with this idea of punishment and the agent of the punishment was the idea of the righteous remnant. This was also connected to the idea of the Lord's mercy. If the Lord had carried his punishment to the extreme, He would have wiped out the Jews. However, the Lord was merciful. Therefore, He used the punishment of being conquered and expelled to sift the Jewish people, to purify them. Those purified would return to the land of their fathers and would serve the Lord with a special zeal. Purified and sifted, they would rebuild the temple and allow the Lord to demonstrate His glory to the world. In this sense, there is almost a type of determinism. Up to now, the people had failed because God had not sufficiently influenced their thoughts and behaviour. However, the Lord would set right the hearts of His people. He would give them a new heart and they would be and remain His people forever.

b) *Explanations in terms of the Lord's plans for Israel in terms of the wider world*

Integrated into this whole idea of the righteous remnant was the idea concerning the role of Jews in the world. In this regard, there seems to be a double message. The Lord is seen as having restored the righteous remnant to their rightful place so that other people would come to glorify the Lord once they saw what He had done for His people.

At the same time, however, the Book of Isaiah also speaks of the time when all those people who do not recognize the suzerainty of the Israelites would be destroyed. Thus, it speaks of the Israelites becoming a light among the nations (Isaiah 49: 6). All nations shall come to their light and their kings to the "brightness of your rising" (Isaiah 60: 2-3). At that time God shall decide for many nations. A utopian society will be ushered in when the sword shall be beaten into ploughshare, nation shall not lift up the sword against nation, and the wolf and the lamb shall feed together. At the same time, the writer states that the "sons of those who afflicted you shall come bowing to you, and all those who despised you (while you were in exile) shall fall prostrate at the soles of your feet" (Isaiah 60:14). Again, your "gates shall be open continually; they shall not be shut day or night, that men may bring to you the wealth of the Gentiles, and their kings in procession. For the nation and kingdom which will not serve you shall perish; and those nations shall be utterly ruined" (Isaiah 60: 11-12).

c) The righteous remnant is to obtain its ultimate reward while under the rule or guidance of the true servant of the Lord.

Generally, the servant of the Lord is seen as a type of David-like figure who will help guide his people and keep them in the ways of the Lord. He is the future ideal leader, or ideal prince. In a sense, he is a savior-like figure who will arrive in a time when the Jews will again please the Lord and as a result will reap the rewards of His blessings.

In summary, the Book of Isaiah's interpretation of the conquest of Judah, the destruction of Jerusalem and the return of the "remnant" gives evidence of the following:

The people of Judah were conquered and dispersed, not because the Israelite God, Yahweh, was weaker than other gods, but to punish them for their sins. This approach is not unique to the recorders of Jewish history. In fact, other ancient peoples used this rationalization at different times to explain why they had gone down to defeat in wars fought against followers of other gods.

Despite the conquest and expulsions, the Jews had the most powerful deity. In fact, He was so powerful that He could use heathen peoples, the followers of other gods, to carry out His plans for His chosen. In this regard, the Israelite God had used the conquest and destruction not merely to punish but also to purify His people.

Purified, they would better achieve God's plan for them:
- they would be a light to the nations;
- at the same time, they would gain power over other nations.
-Their moment of power and glory may not be now. However, it would come in the future, at some time when God would choose to act on behalf of His chosen people.

Therefore, the account in the Book of Isaiah is not unique in the manner in which it records Jewish history and describes the relationship between the Jewish people and their God. It is part of a pattern. This pattern illustrates several characteristics. Of these, the following are extremely significant:

1) Defeat is no indication of a weak God. Rather, it is used by God to punish the people. It is an educational tool used by Him to encourage His chosen to follow Him.

2) In this scheme of things, God frequently sends the people a savior. He is in contact with what God wants and through his special relationship with God helps to save the people, who, because of their own wrongdoings and wrong-headedness, have strayed from the path of the Lord.

3) There is also another theme, which appears in particular in the later part of the Bible. God may punish His people now. However, at some future time He shall leave His anger and take them to Him and reward them.

In the following I will explore each of these themes. I will explore themes one and two separately. However, as theme three is an integral part of the development of either, I will discuss it while exploring the themes of reward and punishment and the concept of the savior.

Recording Historical Events 67

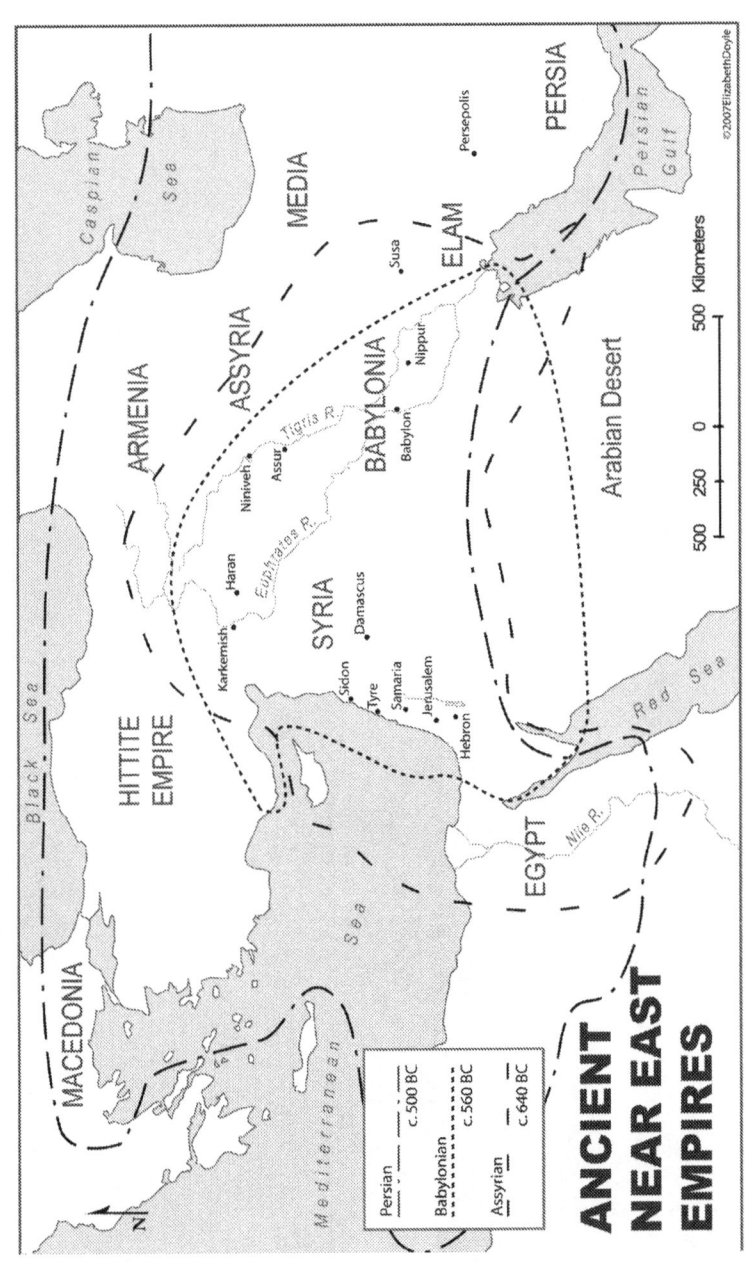

5
Reward and Punishment and God's Relationship with Israel

Reward, Punishment and God's Relationship with Humanity

Integral to the pattern of destruction evidenced in the eradication of the idolaters and aspired to in the Book of Revelation is the biblical view of the human being, of God and the relationship between the two. This relationship is structured largely by reward and punishment, with God punishing people for doing those things He disapproves of and rewarding them for doing the things of which He approves. Reward and punishment, again, derive their potency from the biblical view of humanity and of God and the interaction between the two. Before exploring this interaction and how it relates to the Israelites, I will say a few things about the view of humankind and of God as suggested in the Bible.

The Biblical view of Humanity and its relationship to God

According to the biblical record, God created man and woman in His image and placed them in an earthly Paradise. However, they chose to rebel by eating of the fruit of knowledge, following which God expelled them from Paradise. Upon eating the fruit of knowledge, man and woman lost their purity. They began to give way to their baser instincts, such as greed, sloth, and licentiousness, which God condemned. Places like Sodom and Gomorrah were destroyed because the people had become so sinful as to warrant total obliteration. At times God regretted creating humans, as at the time of the flood, when He had in mind destroying all people because of their sinful nature. However, He did not do so because He found one righteous man, Noah. Of course, the flood suggests that all of humankind except Noah was destroyed, with people after Noah being essentially his descendants.

While the Bible sees people in their sinful state as being worthy of destruction, it also presents another side of humanity, an aspect that in a way is a reflection of God. This is the side the first man and woman revealed while in Paradise. However, with the fall and the expulsion from Paradise, humanity came naturally to be ruled by its lower nature.

The Biblical View of God

God is seen as omnipotent, all-powerful. He is the creator of heaven and earth and all found therein or thereon. At the same time, He has a deep interest in humankind whom He created in His image. In particular, He has an interest in the wellbeing of people and in guiding them to develop their higher nature and suppress their lower nature. An integral part of this guidance consists of using reward and punishment to encourage this development.

Sin and Punishment and the Relationship between Humanity and God

While interested in the general well being of humans, God is in particular interested in their moral nature. Reward and punishment are important, and in many ways the most consistent, means God uses to educate people and have them follow the guidelines He established to raise them to a higher moral plane.

Humans, on the other hand, have an interest in pleasing God, and through this solicitation obtaining His help in negotiating life and gaining those things to which they aspire. At the same time, the human being has an interest in not displeasing God, thereby avoiding punishment. In this way, people and God form a symbiotic relationship, with reward and punishment in many ways structuring the basis of this relationship.

Reward and Punishment and the Relationship between God and Israel

With the founding of Israel, a very significant change occurred in the relationship between humankind and God. Through His

Covenant with the people of Israel, God ceased to be a universal God in many respects. His interaction was confined largely to the people of Israel. That is, they would serve Him. In return, He would bless them. Other people would be involved in this insofar as they would see the wonderful workings of God on behalf of His people and thereby would not only admire the Israelites but also recognize God's greatness. This, at least, is what is suggested by the Covenant.

Through this Covenant, God would love and bless the people of Israel. He would do this in return for their following His commandments and serving Him. However, if they chose not to walk in His ways, then He would punish them. I will explore some of the ways in which God rewarded and punished the Israelites and the part this played in His relationship with Israel and the Israelites' relationship with their God.

Although reward and punishment were used fairly consistently by God to encourage the Israelites to follow His guidance, the manner in which these were bestowed upon the Israelites changes. As these changes reflect and give an indication of the progression from the Holy Land to the New Jerusalem, it would be of interest to look at some of these patterns. Of course, I will concentrate essentially on those changes that give insight into dynamics that help to illustrate how we move from reward and punishment in the temporal sphere to reward and punishment in the eternal sphere.

To illustrate this transformation, I will focus on situations in which God is shown as rewarding or punishing people in different historical situations in which they find themselves. For example, the Psalmist observes that the godless appear to be enjoying plenty. He argues that at times it is difficult to see those who place their trust in God being rewarded in any special way. He continues, however, maintaining that although the wicked appear to prosper, in time God will punish them and reward those who place their trust and faith in Him (see, for example, Psalms 37,112, 125, 129). The Psalmist also speaks of God's wrath against the wicked being carried out in the fullness of time, and of the righteous eventually being rewarded (see, for example, Psalms 75, 94, 98). Similar views are expressed even more succinctly in the Book of Job. Here God is seen as rewarding those who place their faith in Him. Misfortune is attributed to God's testing the faith. The devil, who is seen as seeking to lead people away from God, plays a role. At the same time, the Book argues that those who stand the test and remain faithful to God are doubly rewarded, with Job being given a new family and more riches than he had before his world had been torn apart through the mechanizations of Satan.

It is difficult to determine from the above examples whether they are in essence songs of worship (the Psalms) or part of a morality play (the Book of Job). Furthermore, it is difficult to decipher from the remarks whether the speakers have in mind reward or punishment meted out in this lifetime or in some distant future. The message becomes much clearer when it deals with actual historical situations in which the Jewish people found themselves. Here a specific reward or punishment is often mentioned. The recipient is often an individual or group. Frequently the event discussed relates to historical situations in which, also, different tribal or national groups are involved, permitting us to gain insight into the nature of the reward or punishment not only from the biblical source but also from other sources. This allows one to place events or situations discussed more clearly into a specific context of time and space, thereby permitting one to delineate changes more succinctly.

The Focus on Reward and Punishment in the Temporal Sphere

Although the progression isn't clear-cut, there are certain points in the biblical record where the focus gradually changes from rewards and punishment in the present and in the temporal sphere to the idea of rewards and punishment in the future and, at the same time, in some state experientially unknown to us. This may be observed when we look at the different situations, in particular historical situations, in which the Lord rewarded or punished His people.

This is evident, for example, in the founding of Israel. Thus, Abraham was rewarded for choosing to follow the one true God by laying the basis for the tribal community that came to be Israel. This was continued through Jacob, whose faith was rewarded by the promise that he would found a great people. Both God and Joshua participated in the destruction of the idolaters and the founding of the Holy Land. In fact, God played a significant role in the conquest and destruction. He encouraged Joshua to proceed with the conquest. He gave instructions on how to treat the conquered. He participated in the conquest in that He helped to destroy the protective walls of cities such as Jericho. He offered advice on how to best proceed in the conquest of cities such as Ai. In summary, God acted together with the Israelites to help them gain a territorial place on earth where they could best be assured of His rewards and avoid situations that would result in their being influenced by other peoples and cultures that would lead them away from the religious practices demanded of them, resulting in their being punished.

This pattern of reward and punishment continues in the Book of Judges. Among other things, the Book relates how the Israelites deviated from their worship of their tribal god, Yahweh, which angered Him, causing Him to place them under other peoples. These might conquer and enslave them; or they might rob them of their stored provisions, as had the Midians. The Israelites repented for deviating from their tribal deity, who took pity on them. As a consequence, God had different tribal leaders emerge who displayed their loyalty to Him. Using His help and support, they then rallied the Israelites against outsiders and resolved the problems facing them.

In this regard, Judges follows a fairly consistent pattern. The Israelites fall away from their God and begin to worship other deities. The Lord punishes them. This punishment expresses itself in their being robbed, conquered or suppressed by other peoples. The Israelites repent. The Lord takes pity on them. He sends them a leader who delivers them from their tribulations. All this happens in the temporal sphere, with reward and punishment taking place in the here and now.

Reward and Punishment under the Monarchy

The first Book of Samuel in many ways follows a pattern similar to Judges. Samuel himself was a judge and as such a leader of his people. The Book explores circumstances under which Israelite society moved from being guided by religious leaders to being ruled by kings. The Book of Samuel illustrates the role he had in selecting the first kings, who were chosen largely because the Israelites were clamouring for a king so that they could be like the people around them.

The Israelite king, be this the first king Saul or the most important king, David, was very much seen to be a shepherd to his people. The Kings' works and achievements are described for us not by the rulers themselves but by the Yahwist priesthood. As in Judges, the record unfolds as a part of a moral lesson. While focussing to an extent on the actual event, events tend to be interpreted in terms of the Lord's work on behalf of His people. Good things are attributed to the workings of the Lord on behalf of His people or the kings who pleased Him. Thus, the Lord is described as rewarding faithfulness and punishing deviation from His ordinances. In some instances where a king deviated from the ways of the Lord, victories were also at times attributed to the desire by the God of Israel to prove Himself to His people, despite the failings of the monarch.

The first kings, both Saul and David, were chosen because of their success in fighting Israel's enemies. Thus, Saul was chosen king soon after he won a major victory over Nahash the Ammonite. Saul spent most of his career as king contending against the Philistines as well as other people who at different times warred against the Israelites. The account relates how Saul sought out the advice of Samuel the prophet to divine for him whether he would be victorious in battle. It relates how Saul was successful in defeating the enemies of the Israelites when he followed the Lord's guidance and how he failed when he deviated. Thus, Samuel, as seer who divined God's will, instructed Saul to totally destroy the Amelekites he conquered as well as their livestock as a punishment for their having opposed the Israelites when they took possession of the Holy Land. Saul followed the command only partially: when he defeated the Amelekites from Havilah to Shur, east of Egypt, he utterly destroyed all the people with the edge of the sword. However, he spared Agag the king as well as the best of the livestock (1 Samuel 15: 2-9). As punishment for not obeying the Lord and destroying all these "sinners," the Lord took the kingdom away from Saul and gave it to his rival David.

David continued the fight against the Philistines and was rewarded for his faithfulness to the Lord by the expansion of the territory held by the Israelites. Thus, he re-conquered the cities Saul had lost to the Philistines following his defeat on Mount Gilboa. In these battles, as for example in the Israelite war against the Philistines in the valley of Rephaim (2 Samuel 5: 18-25), the Lord not only advised whom to attack but also how to attack. At the same time, David conquered territory the Israelites did not claim as their inheritance, such as the kingdoms of Moab or Edom. Inhabitants here were either enslaved or paid tribute to the Israelites. At the same time, David united under himself both Israel and Judah. He increased the size of the city of Jerusalem and made plans to build the House of the Lord there, thereby helping to make it the main centre of worship of the God of Israel.

His son, Solomon, expanded upon David's plans. He had the house of the Lord constructed, and undertook many other building projects, both in Jerusalem and in other centres of Judah.[1] To provide a work force for his construction projects, Solomon enslaved all "the people who were left of the Amorites, Hittites, Perizzites, Hivites, and Jebusites, who were not of the children of Israel – that is, their descendants who were left in the land after them, whom the children of Israel had not been able to destroy completely..."(1 Kings 9: 20-21). In particular, Solomon, we are told, was able to channel wealth into the land through gaining control of major trade routes in the Near Middle East. He became especially renowned for his wisdom. Again, this all was attributed to the king's heeding the Lord. At the same time, the decline of his kingdom was prophesied, being seen as a punishment for Solomon's having served deities his wives had brought into the land (1 Kings 11: 32-37).

In many respects, it was because David had won favour in the eyes of the Lord that caused God to also support the work of Solomon, who followed David to the throne. As a reward largely for David's trust and faithfulness, Israel expanded and prospered and, under David and Solomon, attained the height of its glory.

The Prophets, Seers, Reward and Punishment

One of the rewards bestowed upon people such as David, who had succeeded in establishing a direct relationship with God, was that, in most instances, they had been able to tune into what was the will of God and act accordingly, thereby gaining the rewards offered. It seems that few Israelite leaders had this ability and, therefore, were dependent upon the prophets to apprise themselves of God's will. It appears that prophets had always been a part of Israelite society. They were active while Judges ruled Israel, with the high priest, who was also a prophet, acting as both spiritual and secular leader of his people. Once he had divined the will of the Lord, he would seek to direct the people to enable them to gain the Lord's blessings rather than be punished by Him.

With the establishment of the monarchy under Saul, the role of spiritual and secular leader was divided. The prophets, who tended to be part of the religious leadership, served to determine the wishes of the Lord regarding the people of Israel. The king tended to be viewed as the shepherd of his people. The prophet would let the king know what action was right and pleasing in the eyes of the Lord. The choice was then left up to the king to guide the people accordingly. The king and/or the people were then rewarded or punished, depending upon the choices made by the king.

At the same time, the prophet did more than let the monarch know of God's will. He also acted as a type of ambassador of God, who sought to let the monarch know of God's reality and power. This happened in particular while Ahab was king, when prophets such as Elijah and Elisha made a concerted effort to prove to both king and people that the Israelite God was more powerful than the Philistine god Baal, and indeed was the only true God. The performance of magical acts and miracles were an integral part of this process. Thus, the prophet Elijah had fire pour from heaven and consume his sacrifice to show that the Israelite God was more powerful than Baal. There are reports of his ascending directly to heaven to illustrate his closeness to the deity. His disciple, Elisha, also performed many miracles to demonstrate the power of God. As Christ did after him, he fed a mass of people with little food. He cured the ill, raised the dead, and did other things in the Lord's name to illustrate the power of the God of Israel.

Despite such endeavours, related to us in the Book of Kings that deals largely with the attempt by the different prophets to guide the monarchs in the ways of the Lord, there were all too few kings who heeded their counsel. This was true in particular of the monarchs of Israel, which led, eventually, to the destruction of the kingdom and its absorption into the Assyrian empire. As Finkelstein makes clear, it was less true of the Kingdom of Judah, which gave it some hope of avoiding the fate of the kingdom of Israel.[2] Punishment was meted out most frequently through defeats in war. However, at times, even wicked monarchs were given success. Thus, the Lord gave Ahab victory over the Syrians even though Ahab did what was evil in the eyes of the Lord. God granted him victory, however, not because of what Ahab did, but rather to show His power and illustrate His loyalty to the seed of Abraham (1 Kings 20: 13-35). At the same time, the Lord used both Hebrews and non-Hebrews to reward and punish. Thus, he used Hazael, the king of Syria, to punish the Israelites (2 Kings 8: 12-15). He used Jehu, the commander of Israel's forces, to cut from the throne the house of Ahab and punish Ahab's wife Jezebel for the blood of all the servants of the Lord that she had spilled ((2 Kings 9: 7-10). It was the anger of the Lord and the sins of Israel that caused Him to give the Israelites into the hands of the Syrians, and to cut off parts of Israel through Hazael, the King of Syria (2 Kings 10: 32-33; 13:3).

Reward and Punishment in the above and Reward and Punishment as described in the Book of Isaiah

When one looks at God's rewards not only during the time of the monarchy but also prior to this, it becomes evident that these share certain features. That is, they were all granted in time and space. They were granted on earth. More often than not they ensued from specific behaviour of which the Lord approved. For the people, they came in the form of freedom, in particular from foreign rule. For the monarchs, they came largely in the form of victories during military campaigns. This situation altered significantly with the destruction of Jerusalem under Nebuchadnezzar in 587 BC, and the expulsion of leading families of Judah and their return some 50 years later, after Cyrus of Persia had conquered Babylon. Rather than a monarch, a representative of the Persian monarch now ruled Israel. At the same time, the Judean priesthood was given extensive power to direct the religious life of their people.

In this situation, the role of the prophets as well as the nature of their prophecy altered. Whereas, prior to the expulsion, people were for the most part rewarded in the here and now, the Book of Isaiah speaks of rewards at some unknown future time. These rewards would not accrue to the tribal community as a whole, as had generally been the case before, but to the righteous remnant that returned following the Babylonian expulsion.

Also, as Isaiah emphasizes, it was not anything the Israelites had done that allowed the righteous remnant to return. In fact, they had become so sinful that God could justifiably have wiped them out. However, He had not done so. Rather, He had used the destruction of the Temple and the expulsion as a means whereby to punish His people, but then in His mercy had allowed a righteous remnant to return. The Lord allowed them to return because of His great mercy, for the sake of His affection for King David, and also to assure that His experiment with Israel would continue. Thus, greater emphasis tends to be placed on God's mercy and on God's acting on His own rather than through people than was the case before.

Also, the nature of God's rewards and the manner of their bestowal altered. At the time of the founding of Israel, the Lord promised to fight on behalf of the Israelites and bestow all good things upon them in the Holy Land, should they remain faithful to Him. In the Book of Isaiah, the Jews were promised power over the heathens in the world. All they would have to do was retain the faith, their trust in the Lord. It seemed that the Lord, rather than acting through His people, would Himself bring this about.

Reward and Punishment as Described in the Book of Daniel

Another major step from the Holy Land toward the Book of Revelation is taken in the Book of Daniel. This may be observed when one looks at the nature of reward and punishment described therein. As this Book was heavily drawn upon by John in the Book of Revelation and spells out a collective vision of Israelite salvation, I will go into the work in some detail.

While the prophecies of Isaiah, Jeremiah and Ezekiel constituted a response to the exile and the return of the remnant to Judah, the prophecy of Daniel was a response to the attempt by the Greek Seleucid monarch Antiochus IV to force the Jews to worship him as divine. The deification of national leaders has a long history in the ancient world, dating back to the beginning of civilization. It was practised by the Egyptians, where the pharaoh was often seen as divine or as a god. It was practised by the Greeks and Romans, where an emperor often declared himself to be divine. Often this did not involve imposed emperor worship. Some rulers, however, required people to worship them as divine, in part, at times, to help sustain unity in the empire. This practice had little effect on people with many deities, with emperor worship merely adding another deity to the many gods already worshipped. For Jews, however, who recognized only one deity, the practice was tantamount to idolatry. Thus, foreign rulers tended to exempt Israelites from this practice. This was not the case with Antiochus IV, however, who sought to force emperor worship on them.

The Book of Daniel is a product of the Antiochean persecution of the Jews. Almost two centuries had elapsed since Alexander's campaigns had broken Persian power and had inaugurated the Hellenistic period in the eastern Mediterranean world. After Alexander's death the vast empire he had founded was divided amongst dynasties of Macedonian descent. In the second century BC Judah was under the rule of one such dynasty, the Seleucids, who were based in Syria.

Deviating from the religious tolerance that characterized most governments in the Greek-speaking world, in the 160s BC the Seleucid monarch Antiochus IV Epiphanes launched a massive attack upon Judaism in an attempt to force the Jews to worship him as a god. In 169 BC, his forces, entering the Temple in Jerusalem, stole cultic ornaments and stripped the building of its gold decorations. Two years later, they pillaged and burned Jerusalem itself. Many of its inhabitants were killed; others were enslaved. Jewish religious observances and customs were forbidden. The cult of the Syrian god, Baal Shamen, replaced that of Yahweh in the Temple, with a new altar being superimposed on the old. Here, taboo animals, pigs, were sacrificed. Altars to pagan gods were set up in the provinces, and everywhere offerings had to be carried out in honour of the king, with royal officials assuring that this was done.

The right that the Jews had traditionally enjoyed, to live according to their own religion, was thereby abolished. Rather than subject themselves to these conditions, many Jews chose to fight. This brought on the Maccabean uprising, the liberation of the Temple in 164 BC, and the restoration of the old cult. Soon after, the Jewish community's traditional rights were restored. The Book of Daniel was written in this environment. The work records the activities of a Jew by the name of Daniel. Although some of the accounts were prepared at the time of the Maccabean conflict, the apocalyptic passages (which were likely prepared by more than one author) appear to have been written between 169 and 165 BC.[3]

Chapter Two of the Book of Daniel recounts a dream in which King Nebuchadnezzar saw a huge image with a golden head, and breasts and arms of silver. Its belly and thighs were of bronze, its large legs of iron, and it feet of both iron and terracotta. As Nebuchadnezzar watched the image, a stone hewn from a mountain fell and struck the feet of the image, shattering them. Thereupon, the entire image disintegrated, without leaving a trace. However, the stone expanded into a mountain, to fill the entire earth. Nebuchadnezzar invited the wise men of Babylon to explain the dream to him. None could. Then Daniel was called upon to explain the dream. Receiving a vision from God, Daniel not only told the king what he had dreamt but also explained the dream's meaning.

According to Daniel, the golden head represented the king himself. The silver and bronze parts of the being represented future kingdoms, all of them inferior to that of Babylon. Daniel was primarily interested in the iron legs and the feet of iron and terracotta, which represented the fourth kingdom. It would suffer from internal weakness. Just as iron and terracotta are incompatible, its attempts to bind its different segments together through dynastic marriages would end in failure, which was no doubt a reference to the problematic relations between the Syrian Seleucids and the Egyptian Ptolemies. Just as shattering iron destroys all things, this kingdom would break and shatter the whole earth. Daniel was, of course, foreseeing the history of Alexander's empire and its successor states. "At the end of this age," God would intervene by establishing a kingdom that would shatter and make an end to all other kingdoms, while it would endure forever. The stone, in fact, represented this kingdom, which would be universal and everlasting.

The idea of world empires, or "kingdoms," one succeeding the other, suggested by Daniel when he discusses the four beasts emerging from the sea, was common in the ancient Near East. One empire is represented by a lion with eagle wings, another by a bear-like being, and another a four-headed winged leopard. Daniel concentrates on the fourth beast:

> After this I saw... a fourth beast, dreadful and terrible, exceedingly strong. It had huge iron teeth; it was devouring, breaking in pieces, and trampling the residue with its feet. It was different from all the beasts that were before it, and it had ten horns. I was considering the horns, and there was another horn, a little one coming up among them, before whom three of the first horns were plucked out by the roots. And there, in this horn, were eyes like the eyes of a man, and a mouth speaking pompous words (Daniel 7: 7-8).

The appearance of the little horn suggests the end of time, when God makes His appearance as "the Ancient of Days." White-haired, white-robed, sitting on a throne of fire, and surrounded by the heavenly host, He administers justice. Upon examining the books in which are recorded each person's actions, God judges the fourth beast as wanting. It is then killed and its body consumed by fire. Following this, "one like the son of man" appears "with the clouds of heaven." The Ancient of Days grants him sovereignty everlasting, requiring all nations and peoples to serve him.

Although this supposedly takes place in heaven, the author repeatedly suggests that it in fact transpires on earth. Thus, the beasts arise out of the sea, which traditionally was seen as the symbol of chaos in conflict with the God-given order in the world and the universe. The beasts emerge on land trampled on by the fourth beast, suggesting Judah.[4] The Book further suggests that God's throne, from which He will judge humankind, is also set up in Judah. The four segments of the image, like the four beasts, symbolize the four imperial powers that ruled over the Jews, "with the fourth beast, Alexander's empire and its successor states, so much worse than all its predecessors."[5]

The aim of the Book was to encourage the Jewish people to stand firm in the face of persecution. God is more powerful than the Seleucids. In time, He will judge the Seleucid kingdom and condemn it to destruction. At the same time, he will place the whole earth under the power of "one like the son of man," who will never be dethroned. As such, "the 'one like a son of man' must be either a symbol of 'the saints of the Most High' or their representative. In either case he embodies the sense of election, the certainty of future vindication and exaltation of the Jews - or rather, of the Jews for whom the author(s) of Daniel wrote."[6]

In many respects, visions and ideas suggested in the Book of Isaiah are expanded to another level of abstraction in the Book of Daniel. Daniel speaks not only of the end of time, but of the establishment of a kingdom and of a state of being in which people will live forever. Not only will those still living be granted everlasting life. All the people who died in the faith, those Jews who died without giving up their beliefs, will be resurrected to live in eternal blessedness. They will rule over the Gentiles forever. But Jews who did not keep the faith will suffer eternal punishment. As such, reward and punishment, while apparently being dealt out in this earth, will be everlasting. Right thought and right behaviour are still rewarded, and wrong thought and behaviour punished. For the Jews, however, these will have everlasting consequences.

In all the above, certain concepts remain constant and others alter. The belief that God is all-powerful remains. He continues to punish evil and reward good. God's major concern is still with the Jewish community. However, He makes a strict division between those who remain true to the faith and those who don't. While they remain on earth, those who don't remain faithful will be punished forever. Those who remain true to the faith will not only be blessed but will live in eternal blessedness. At the same time, they will rule over the Gentiles, these not being part of the larger plan of God's salvation as envisaged by Daniel.

The "saints (or holy ones) of the Most High" are in turn to be identified with the Jews. They will inherit whatever belonged to the pagan empires. Furthermore, each pagan empire exercised its rule until crushed by a successor. The kingdom of Daniel's Jews, however, "shall never pass to another people, it shall shatter and make an end of all these kingdoms, while it shall itself endure for ever and ever."[7] This future empire (which will also be the kingdom of God) will be terrestrial, like the pagan empires preceding it. In fact, it will emerge with the re-consecration of the Temple in Jerusalem that Antiochus had desecrated. Nevertheless, it will differ from, and in many ways be the opposite of, empires that preceded it. Prior to its emergence, justice and righteousness could be fully obtained only in heaven. With its establishment, these would be accessible on earth as well. In fact, the divine order on earth would correspond to that in heaven. The Jews, who would be in control of this kingdom, would differ from Jews of the past. "The very phrase 'people of the saints of the Most High' hints at a people wholly without sin and wholly reconciled with God; and so does the association with the awe inspiring figure of 'one like a son of man.'"[8] Therefore, their "community of 'holy ones' on earth... will correspond to the angelic 'holy ones' in Heaven. And whereas the kingdoms symbolized by the beasts were in their day so many embodiments of purely human, political power... these denizens of the coming kingdom will be vehicles of divine power."[9]

Divine judgment, however, will precede the establishment of this empire of saints. This will determine the future both of the Seleucid Empire and of the individual Jew. Following the overthrow and destruction of Antiochus, Jews who have remained faithful, all those who have their names "written in the book" - will not have to suffer further. In fact, the Book concludes with the prophecy that "many of those who sleep in the dust of the earth shall awake, some to everlasting life, some to shame and everlasting contempt" (Daniel 12: 2).

From the above it appears that keepers of the Israelite record were not so much interested in conscientiously documenting the historical record as they were in using the record to keep alive the faith in a deity that had chosen them as a special people. At the same time, the historical record was written to keep alive their faith in the power of this deity. The heathen may triumph in the present and in the near future. However, at some point in time, God will reveal His power on behalf of His people and place them in the position to which they are entitled because of their faith in Him.

As in Isaiah, the Book of Daniel speaks of the reward coming at some point in the future. However, the work expands significantly on the nature of this reward. All those who remain faithful will be rewarded. The Jews who had died in the faith would be resurrected. Along with the "true" Jews who were still alive, they would not only live forever under ideal circumstances, but would also rule over the Gentiles. Jews who have betrayed the faith, on the other hand, would be punished forever.

The visions of Daniel raised the anticipated rewards for the Jews who kept the faith to another level of abstraction. At the same time, Daniel introduced the concept of resurrection combined with eternal reward and punishment. Neither had appeared in Scripture prior to this. In fact, Cohn observes that the concept of eternal reward and punishment described in the Book of Daniel "has no parallel in the Hebrew Bible: it marks a decisive break with the traditional Israelite notion of death. The prospect of Sheol, 'the pit,' 'the land of oblivion,' that lay before the righteous and unrighteous alike, is replaced by a very different prospect: at the end of the great consummation the dead are to be resurrected, judged and either rewarded or punished."[10] Before discussing these views further, including their possible origin, it would be useful to examine the idea of savior, of the messiah, as he is presented in the biblical record.

6
Changes in the Israelite View of the Messiah or Savior, and the Progression from the Holy Land to the New Jerusalem

To this point, we have looked at God rewarding people by communicating directly with them and then rewarding them if they followed His dictates. We have looked at God communicating with people through the use of prophets and visionaries who notified the Israelites of His will and then rewarded them if they heeded it. In all these situations, God tended to work through people under relatively normal circumstances. At times, however, the community faced particularly trying circumstances, crises in which it made a special effort to seek the Lord's help. On such occasions, the Lord frequently brought to the fore special persons to help the community deal with the situation. Such people were seldom prophets, because prophets tended to warn of danger, expecting others to act. Generally, he or she warned the ruler that goals he was pursuing displeased the Lord and would result in punishment. Saviors, unlike prophets, were used by God to become involved in direct action in the interest of the elect. With the help of God, they generally embarked upon dangerous undertakings, often considered to be humanly impossible, to save the community from tribulation.

Early Saviors

Soon after the conquest of the Holy Land, the Israelites deviated from their worship of their tribal god, Yahweh, causing Him to become angry with them. As a result, He at times placed them under the control of other people. At other times, as in the case of the Midians, He permitted other peoples to rob them of their stored provisions. Realizing the error of their ways, the Israelites repented for deviating from Yahweh, who thereupon took pity on them and sent them a savior through Gideon, who liberated them from the Midians.

Another example of an early savior was Samson. Although he did not deliver the Israelites from the Philistines, he nevertheless gave them courage to stand up to them, and, through this, gain victory over the foe.

Kings who acted as Saviors

The idea of the savior also arises in the Book of Kings. Thus, we read that the anger of the Lord and the sins of Israel caused Him to give the Israelites into the hands of Hazael, King of Syria (2 Kings 13: 3). Yet, when Jehoahaz, the king of Israel, sought the Lord because of His people's suffering, the Lord gave the Israelites a savior so that they escaped from the hands of the Syrians and could dwell in their homes as formerly (2 Kings 13: 4-5). On another occasion, when the king of Israel repented, and also because of his bond with Israel, the Lord sent the Israelites a savior through King Jehoash. Although Jehoash did what was evil in the eyes of the Lord, the Lord had compassion on the Israelites because of the covenant He had with Abraham, Isaac, and Jacob, and Jehoash took from the Syrians the cities that Hazael, the king of Syria, had conquered (2 Kings 13: 10-11, 22-24).

The Idea of the Offspring of David as a Savior

The idea of a savior of the people of Israel at some future time started to play a dominant role in the Israelite historical record in particular after the Babylonian destruction of Jerusalem and the return of the exiles. Thus, the Book of Isaiah speaks of a savior of Israel at the end of time, who will be of the house of David (Isaiah 11: 1-13). Jeremiah states this even more clearly when he remarks that at some future time the Lord "will raise up for David a righteous Branch, and he shall reign as king and deal wisely, and shall execute justice and righteousness in the land. In his days Judah will be saved, and Israel will dwell securely" (Jeremiah 23: 5-8).

The Son of Man as a Savior

The savior image takes on a pronouncedly mythological form in the Book of Daniel. Thus, Daniel speaks of the Son of Man who at the end of time will enter into battle against the beast. Inevitably, the victory of the Son of Man will result in the victory of those Israelites who have not lost faith in their deity.

Unlike earlier saviors, the Son of Man is a vague, all-powerful figure, who fights against an equally vague and all-powerful beast. He will not so much lead the people to gain their salvation; rather, he will be that all-powerful force conducting war on behalf of the righteous. He will vanquish the forces of evil and initiate a time when the righteous of Israel will not only live forever but will have dominion over the Gentiles.

Christ the Messiah

The next major change in the idea of a savior influencing the movement from the Holy Land to the New Jerusalem may be observed when one looks at Christ in the context of the Israelite messiah tradition. Christ as savior is at different times depicted in the guise of the various saviors who preceded him. As in other cases, the concept of Christ as savior, as the messiah figure in general, grew largely out of the experience of Israel's helplessness in the face of a foreign power. The Israelite priesthood, especially the prophets, following the Babylonian conquest, looked in particular to the offspring of David to bring a possible savior. It is not surprising, therefore, that the followers of Jesus, when witnessing His miracles, fit Him into this tradition - the tradition of the messiah who would arise from the seed of David.

A number of factors influenced the followers of Christ to view Him as the ultimate messiah, the savior of Israel. These included the miracles He performed, such as waking the dead, multiplying loaves of bread, and healing the sick - all miracles that did not differ significantly from those performed previously. Elisha, for example, was also described as having done miracles such as bringing the dead back to life (2 Kings 8:1). Christ's miracles, as well as His ambiguous references to Himself as the Son of Man, couldn't help but instil in His followers as well as in other Israelites the belief that He in fact might be the person they were waiting for, who would free them from foreign rule.

Of course, Christ never offered the Jews this type of salvation. He wasn't concerned with freeing the Israelites from foreign rule. Nor was He concerned with any policy that would make the Israelites stand out in some special way so that they would receive the benefits God would bestow upon them as His special people. Jesus' focus on the earthly life being lived to gain rewards or punishment in the afterlife does not at all appear in the first part of the Bible. There people were punished or rewarded during their earthly existence. In fact, Israel was established largely to assure that the chosen of Yahweh could best follow the rules and carry out the practices demanded of them by Him so that they could gain His rewards and escape His punishment on earth. These punishments involved defeat in war, or expulsion from the land God had promised unto them. This affected not only the individual but also the community as a whole. The belief in punishment after death does not appear in the Old Testament until later - for example, in the Book of Daniel. Here Daniel speaks of the dead rising and those people who remain true to the faith going to their eternal rewards and those who do not remain true going to their eternal punishment. This contrasts sharply with the view of the Psalmist, who writes that man "is like the beasts that perish" (Psalm 49: 20). He returns to the dust. At the same time, ancient Israelites believed that life could continue beyond death. It was this belief that caused Saul to have Samuel called up from the land of the dead so that he might prophecy to him the outcome of a war he was planning against the Philistines (I Samuel 28: 8-20). However, the afterlife was not seen as the time when man would be rewarded or punished for the type of life he lived on earth.

Both Saul and the Psalmist saw man as earth-centred. Christ, on the other hand, focuses on life as a preparation for the eternal judgment and the afterlife. This is true to some extent of the apocalyptic vision in Daniel, where those who remain faithful are rewarded at the time when the Lord will take it upon himself to wipe out the representatives of evil and bring the triumph of the good. Daniel, however, still speaks of the faithful remnant of Israel - those who remained true to the faith and didn't give in to the idolatrous demands of the Seleucids - being rewarded as a

Changes in the Israelite View 89

collectivity. Christ speaks of each individual making a moral choice between doing those things that are pleasing unto God or doing those things that are condemned by him. While there are certain rewards for doing good in the present, this is not Christ's focus. Rather, He emphasizes the rewards people will reap in heaven for their good deeds. Those who do evil will reap punishment in the afterlife, with reward or punishment being bestowed upon the individual rather than the group.

Whereas the traditional Israelite savior acted essentially to save the Jewish community, Christ's message had relevance to each man, woman and child on earth. In this way, the idea of the Israelite savior became relevant for all of humankind. By making the message of salvation applicable to everyone, Christ expanded the Israelite message of salvation to include not only an elect tribal group. In this way Christ's message, while rooted in Judaism, at the same time is completely contrary to the very idea of an elect ethnicity. Rather, it defines electedness on the basis of individual belief, and behaviour ensuing from it.

Several factors appear to have contributed to this change. One was the hopelessness of the situation in which the chosen people had found themselves since the establishment of the Holy Land. The Assyrians had conquered them. The Babylonians had conquered them. They were freed from captivity by the Persians and allowed to return home. The prophets might well talk about God using Nebuchadnezzar and Cyrus as His instruments. They might well talk about God using Cyrus to effect their return. However, Cyrus made it quite plain in his prayer to Marduk, the Babylonian god, that when returning the different peoples and the different gods to their homes, he was trying to gain the favour of all gods, and in particular the favour of the Babylonian god Marduk.

More than a promise, the prophetic writings bring to mind a plea, an attempt at reassurance despite evidence to the contrary. The Israelites should not lose faith. Their deity is the greatest of gods. He will eventually lead them to triumph. At the same time, rather than spokesmen of peace, they are spokesmen of a suppressed aggression. They speak of a lion and a lamb lying down together. They speak of other aliens worshipping in the house of God. At the same time, they suggest that their deity will crush those peoples who will not bow to the Israelites once God manifests His full power and glory. The Israelites will not crush these peoples. Rather, God will do so. It is a voice of a people who have lost their ability to control their destiny. Their war god no longer acts on their behalf in the present. The time of Joshua when God uses His people to destroy others is past. Even the time of David, when God used the king of the chosen to effect His great deeds, was past. God, the prophets prophesied, would eventually act on Israel's behalf. He would bring them victory. The Book of Daniel is essentially a continuance of this train of thought. However, Daniel also introduces new ideas. He promises eternal life to those Jews who retain the faith. At the same time, God threatens those who lose the faith with eternal punishment.

As in the case of the prophets, Daniel's is a plea that the Israelites not lose the faith. The God of Israel will triumph. He is the most powerful of gods. As in the case of Isaiah and Jeremiah, Daniel sees this triumph, not in the present, but in the future, at the end of time. At the end of time the Israelites who keep the faith will triumph, will live eternally and will be given eternal dominance over the heathens. Those Israelites who do not keep the faith will be condemned to eternal suffering. Not only those living will experience this. The graves will open and the faithful Jews will go to their reward while the unfaithful will be punished eternally.

In many respects, Christ represents a loss of faith in the belief in the Israelite idea of collective salvation. This essentially returns us to the days of Abraham, when the individual rather than the community was seen to be God's primary concern. However, unlike Abraham who sought and was granted rewards on earth, Christ spoke of rewards after death, of reward or punishment accruing to each individual. This is in many ways a radical transformation in the role occupied by earlier saviors in Israelite society. In fact, there is little that Christ the Savior has in common with such earlier saviors. The only savior He has something in common with is the Son of Man savior described in the Book of Daniel. However, the Son of Man is more of a warrior than is Christ. Christ speaks of a coming judgment when both the righteous and the unrighteous shall be judged. He doesn't speak of Himself as the agent who will do battle and vanquish the forces of wickedness.

In fact, in many respects, the Book of Revelation combines the image of Christ the Savior as He is presented in the Gospels with the Son of Man concept as expressed in the Book of Daniel. While using the Son of Man image as found in the Book of Daniel, the Book of Revelation expands on this and at the same time alters it. In the Book of Revelation we do not have the slain Lamb merely fighting some vague force. Rather, we have the slain Lamb fighting the Antichrist and all the forces associated with him. In one respect, John makes use of images found in the Book of Enoch where a great sword is given to the white sheep, symbolic representatives of the people of Israel, who proceed against all the beasts of the field in order to kill them (Enoch 90:19). Again, the writer greatly expands on earlier concepts. The final result is that we have great cosmic battles, the end consequence of which is the salvation of all the followers of Christ, including those who come from among the children of Israel. Jews who have forsaken their religious traditions or are not followers of Christ, as well as other non-believers, are destined to hell.

7
The Historical Experience, Reward and Punishment, and the Savior

The historical experience of the Israelites, their interpretation of this experience in the context of reward and punishment, and their view of the savior or messiah, are closely linked. Central to this experience is the belief in an all-powerful God and, as importantly, God's response to prayer.

When after one has sought favour with the most powerful deity in heaven and on earth, who determines the fate of all of humankind, only to find that one's supplication had gone unheeded, one is inevitably left with the question: why did God not grant me what I had prayed for? In the case of a group, it might well ask: why did our God not grant us what we asked for? He certainly could have done so. After all, He is the most powerful of gods.

People might find an excuse in all sorts of things. They might tell themselves that God was asleep or, perhaps, He was preoccupied with other matters. All such suppositions limit the deity and make his actions suspect. Having the deity structuring his actions in terms of reward and punishment has several advantages over these excuses. It helps preserve the belief that the divinity is omniscient as well as omnipresent. This is extremely important, in part because it imparts to the deity's priesthood a significant role as mediators between the divinity and the community. More significant, perhaps, is that it allows the supplicant the opportunity to manipulate the deity, thereby placing a certain degree of control of the divine into the hands of the worshipper. In particular, it helps the believer negotiate his or her way through an especially threatening environment.

In a sense, through supplication one can call upon the deity at one's convenience. Religious rituals intended to approach and satisfy the deity provide a way of accessing its power. Religious laws provide guidance for this, letting one know what the deity expects so that one can do the things that bring rewards and avoid punishment. At the same time, religious rules provide a way of uniting the community in the attempt to realise group goals. They provide explanations when things do not turn out as expected or hoped for. During darkest hours of foreign dominance and repression, these gave the Jewish people the reassurance that the course of events would eventually turn out to their advantage. All they had to do was believe and try a little harder.

The messiah or potential leader played an important role in this regard. He provided a focus and rallying cry around which to keep such hopes alive. He provided a focus for marshalling and uniting the community in a common purpose. Insofar as he was successful, he served as the bridge between the community and its faith, working to direct group energy and the forces in the larger universe toward realizing community goals.

In particular, the idea of David and the house of David served a useful purpose in this regard. King David provided an example that pleasing the Israelite deity was possible. At the same time, he provided a vision of the success that might be attained through faith in the God of Israel. The idea of the Son of Man served a somewhat similar function. It is rather interesting that he appeared or the idea of the Son of Man was formulated at the time when the Jews no longer could measure their success or failures in terms of what happened in Palestine itself. They had become a part of world empires. They could be successful in their homeland and still find themselves under someone else's suzerainty. Therefore the ideal Israelite leader had to realize this expansive role. He would lead the Israelites to victory over the Gentiles not only in Israel but also in the entire world. This expressed the power of the universal deity. At the same time, it took cognizance of the geopolitical environment in which the Jewish people found themselves as a segment of a larger world empire. In this situation, the Son of Man would give the Israelites power over the Gentiles not only in the Holy Land but also in the entire world. At the same time, he was a fitting counterbalance to the egoism of the earthly ruler who insisted on having himself worshipped as a god.

In a sense, Christ as the hoped-for messiah combines both the idea of the savior who will emerge from the House of David to save Israel (stressed in both Isaiah and Jeremiah) and of the semi-divine Son of Man who would usher in a new world for the

Israelites. As in the case of the prophets, His followers looked to Him for signs that He was in fact empowered by the tribal deity. This would show that God had sent the Israelites a savior for whom the community was yearning. This would also show that this savior would be able to effect the changes the community desired but was unable to bring about on its own.

Of course, the salvation that Christ spoke of was totally different from the salvation for which community leaders were yearning. They wanted to be rid of the foreign yoke and, perhaps, wield the power over their foreign rulers that these foreigners were exercising over them. Christ, on the other hand, offered salvation, not for any collectivity, but for the individual. He offered salvation, not in the earthly realm, but salvation from hell in the afterlife.

In some respects, the Book of Revelation presents us with a scenario of how the salvation offered by Christ would occur. It offers us an idea as to the time when it would come about. Also, it provides an insight into what the new order that will be ushered in through the triumph of God through Christ will be like. That is, it prophesies the coming of the new heaven and the new earth. It prophesies the coming of a New Jerusalem more splendid than any that preceded it. In it, the saved will live in eternal bliss, while the damned will suffer eternal pain in hell.

The salvation for Jews who remain true to the faith or for believers in Christ will be wrought through God, acting through the Lamb, who in many ways is the ultimate war god. Of course, any aggressive tendencies he may have are projected onto Satan and his followers. The idea we are left with is that any excesses, no matter how horrendous, are permissible in the cause of destroying that which is designated as "evil" so as to bring about the salvation of the righteous. In many ways we have the return to the scenario of the Book of Joshua where the destruction of those designated as evil is permissible because it is carried out in the cause of the salvation of the elect. However, in Revelation, the struggle is universal rather than local or regional. It affects the whole universe. The salvation aspired to is not a Paradise-like existence on earth but rather eternal bliss. To achieve it, the enemies of the people of the light are not killed but are condemned to eternal punishment. It may be of interest to explore further some of the ideas and concepts that led to this evolution.

8
From Earthly Event to Apocalyptic Vision—An Evolution of Beliefs and Concepts

The first holocaust relates to an event that happened in time and space. Although we do not know to what extent it was actually carried out, the evidence suggests that we are dealing here with an historical occurrence, and with behavior that the Israelites or a group of Israelites exhibited toward the original inhabitants of Canaan. The Apocalypse described in the Book of Revelation did not actually take place. Rather, John prophesies that it will take place. Apocalypse means disaster, cosmic catastrophe, and the end of the world.

It may be of interest to explore what influences may have contributed to the images of creation and destruction that Daniel suggests but which are described in more detail in the Book of Revelation. There is little to suggest that they had their origin solely in the Israelite tradition as expressed in the Bible. Thus, the Bible speaks of God being angry with man at the time of Noah and contemplating his destruction. At the same time, the Bible makes mention of God having destroyed Sodom and Gomorrah because of the multitude of sins their inhabitants committed. In the one case, God contemplates destroying all of humankind on earth and in the other he destroys people in certain locales. There is no mention at all of an afterlife, nor of reward or punishment in the afterlife.

The idea of a final destruction of the world also arose among other people. Thus, Greek stoic philosophers identified the original elements of our universe as fire. They saw the universe as passing through cycles of conflagration in which everything would be destroyed by fire, the whole process being similar to birth, death and rebirth. The universe would be consumed by fire and then renewed again, with the conclusion of one destruction ushering in a rebirth, the cycle continuing forever. Some Greek philosophers, such as Seneca who died in AD 65, didn't envisage merely a process of destruction and renewal. Seneca maintained that there would be a final conflagration through a universal fire, which would usher in a new, just, and happy world.

Numerous other apocalyptic prophecies also envisaged the annihilation of the existing world and its re-creation. Greek myth mentions Deucalion, the son of Prometheus, who with his wife, Pyrrha, survived the destruction wrought when Zeus flooded the earth, and recreated the new men and women of Greece. Berosus, a Babylonian priest in the third century BC, wrote about the Chaldean doctrine of the Great Year. While envisaging the universe to be eternal, it maintains that the world is destroyed and re-created every Great Year, with such a year lasting, perhaps, several millennia. Nordic myths speak of the world being destroyed by fire and flood, after monsters slay the Nordic gods at Ragnarok. The world-tree, Ygdrasil, however, survives to bear a new man, Lif, and a new woman, Lifthrasir. They bring into being the next human race. The American ghost dance religion of the late nineteenth century envisaged the destruction of the world as we know it and its replacement by a paradise-like world.

While the apocalyptic view of destruction and regeneration appears in many different cultures and is fairly universal, the view that has such a process becoming an integral part of the destruction and punishment of a particular group and the reward of another group by sending them to hell is less common. In fact, it was first clearly enunciated and became part of a religious system in Zoroastrianism, a religion that was introduced into Persia over a thousand years before the birth of Christ, and flourished there and in neighbouring lands for some twelve centuries. According to Zoroaster, the fate of the world and the universe is divided into four 3000-year segments, where Ahura Mazda, the force of light and goodness in the universe, struggles against Ahriman, the spirit of darkness and evil. The fourth trilenium begins with the birth of Zoroaster, and the end of each of its millennia is marked by the appearance of savior figures, each a godlike prophet, each miraculously conceived by a virgin, each renovating the world and helping to perfect humankind.

The third and last such savior, an offspring of Zoroaster who like the previous Zoroasters would be born of a virgin, would usher in a new creation. The World Savior would come in glory; a great ordeal by fire and molten metal would follow his arrival, which would herald the final battle in which the forces of Ahura Mazda, the forces of light and goodness in the universe led by Zoroaster, would do battle with and conquer the forces of Ahriman, the forces of evil. Following this, the dead would be resurrected. The living and the dead would then be judged. The followers of Ahura Mazda, or the good, would go to heaven. Those who had done evil would plunge into hell. Here they would remain for three days until they were purified in the manner in which metal is purified by means of fire. Purified, they would then join the others in the service of Ahura Mazda. In this renewed heaven and earth, there would be neither death nor suffering, which were brought about through the workings of the evil spirit, Ahriman. With him no longer active, people would live in a paradise-like environment. Of all the above prophecies of the end of time, the transformations described in the Book of Daniel and especially in the Book of Revelation come closest to those envisaged by Zoroaster.

At the same time, both the Book of Daniel and Revelation grew out of a multitude of prophecies of violence threatened by Jewish prophets, in particular following the destruction of Jerusalem. Thus, Zechariah 14:12 describes the plague with which the Lord would smite Jerusalem's enemies: "Their flesh shall dissolve while they stand on their feet, their eyes shall dissolve in their sockets, and their tongues shall dissolve in their mouths." Joel, again, speaks of the day of the Lord that is near at hand (2:10): thick darkness, devouring fire, devastation, and running hither and thither. "The earth quakes.... The heavens tremble. The sun and moon grow dark, and the stars diminish in their brightness." The Book of Daniel is part of this tradition and the Book of Revelation grew out of this tradition that saw the Israelites, or at least those Israelites who remained faithful to God, being rewarded and the enemies of Israel being punished or totally destroyed.

This suggests that the vision of salvation presented in the Book of Revelation grew not only out of the Jewish experience. It also evolved from influences of groups interacting with the Jewish community, with the Jews not only absorbing ideas and beliefs held by their neighbors but also expanding upon and developing them to suit their own needs and condition.

This may also be observed, for example, when looking at the idea of Christ the Son of God. In particular ancient polytheistic societies held the view that their rulers were the sons of one god or another. Thus, Roman and Greek rulers at different times saw themselves sons of one of their gods. At times, as in the case of Antiochus, they expected themselves to be worshiped as gods. The Israelites never went to these extremes, and the Pharisees appear to have considered the very suggestion of Christ claiming to be a son of the Almighty as a sign of blasphemy, which was one reason why they considered Him worthy of crucifixion. At the same time, the Book of Samuel has the prophet Nathan relating the following concerning King David: "I will be his Father, and he shall be My son" (II Sam. 7:14). Elsewhere, the prophet Hosea, repeating an earlier reference to the Israelites as the "children of the Lord" (Deut. 14:1), calls the people of Israel the "sons of the living God" (Hos. 1:10).

The depiction of Christ as the Son of God born of a virgin and Christ the Lamb battling the Antichrist shows the influence of these different traditions. Thus, the virgin birth of Christ shows the influence of Zoroastrianism, where the different Zoroasters were seen to be brought into the world by virgins. At the same time, Luke's depiction of Christ as the Son of God shows in particular Roman influence. Not only that, Marcus Borg sees Luke's account regarding Christ's divine origin as being a direct challenge to Roman imperial theology. According to this theology, the emperor was considered to be a son of god because of his divine descent. Taking root with Caesar, who was considered to be a descendant of the god Venus through her son Aeneas, this theology was fully developed by the time of Caesar Augustus, Rome's greatest emperor. He was said to have been fathered by the god Apollo, who impregnated Augustus's mother, Atia, while she slept. Atia's husband was notified of this divine conception through a dream in which he saw the sun rise from her womb. As signs of Augustus's divine origin, his life was characterized by spectacular deeds.[1]

The main gift that Augustus was believed to have brought to his people was peace following years of warfare. Borg sees Luke as placing Christ's birth story within this historical context to argue that, rather than the emperor Augustus and his successors,

From Earthly Event to Apocalyptic Vsion 101

Christ is the true and only Son of God. As such, he will bring both peace and justice to earth.[2] He will usher in, not only a new society, but the Kingdom of God.[3]

The concept of the Kingdom of God appears at different times in scripture. Thus, the concept of the Kingdom of the Lord is used to describe the enthronement of Solomon (1 Chron. 28:5). Another time, the concept is used in reference to the dynastic war between Abijah and Jeroboam (2 Chron. 13:8). The only other reference to the Kingdom of God (or the Kingdom of Yahweh) prior to 70 BC is found in the Psalms of Solomon, written between 63 BC and the Temple's destruction. Psalm 17:13 states that "the kingdom of our God is forever over the nations in judgment." The reference suggests, however, that it came into being during the Second Temple period, that is, after the return from Babylon. It is found in the same Psalm in which the term "messiah" is used with reference to David's descendant who will purify Jerusalem and subject the Gentiles to his rule at the end of time.[4]

The evidence suggests that all the kingdoms referred to in the above were centered on earth. It is somewhat unclear whether the Kingdom of God of which Christ spoke would be established on earth or in heaven. That is because reports by Christ's disciples such as Mark, Luke, Matthew, or John, who bore witness to his life and teachings, are unclear. This leaves scholars such as Marcus Borg to claim that the Kingdom of God promised by Christ would be established on earth rather than in heaven. At the same time, he asserts that the statement by the Apostle John that believers in Jesus will be rewarded with eternal life does not refer to the afterlife, but rather to "life of the age to come," on earth.[5] Borg is able to pursue this line of argument because concepts such as "eternal life" and "life of the age to come" are somewhat ambiguous in the gospels of Mark, Luke, Matthew, and John. The Book of Revelation, however, has little such ambiguity. Here, the writer John makes it quite clear that Christ the Lamb will not usher in the Kingdom of God in time and space. Like Zoroaster fighting Ahriman on behalf of Ahura Mazda, Christ the Lamb will usher in the Kingdom of God, not on earth or in time and space, but in the afterlife and in heaven. True believers will be rewarded with heaven and non-believers with hell. Those in heaven will enjoy bliss and eternal life, while non-believers will go to hell where punishment is eternal.

The idea of a parent sacrificing a child, in particular a beloved child, an innocent child, as atonement for transgressions, appears to go back to a very ancient tradition. Mention is made of it in the Old Testament, where Abraham is about to offer his son as a sacrifice. The example also gives an idea of child sacrifice moving to animal sacrifice. Abraham was about to sacrifice his son when he saw a ram that had gotten entangled in some brush, and he offered it up to God instead of his beloved son. Of course, Judaism appears to have evolved out of an older religious tradition that involved child sacrifice. Once animal sacrifice came to substitute for child sacrifice, it was in particular the lamb, the symbol of innocence, which was often sacrificed. So, the idea of a son being offered as a sacrifice is an old one, as is also the identification between a lamb and an innocent child being offered in sacrifice.

The idea that individuals willingly sacrificing their own life for others could serve as an antidote to sin was not new to the Israelite tradition at the time of Christ. Thus, the Maccabees who had martyred themselves in opposing Antiochus became, "as it were, a ransom for the sin of our nation" (4 Macc. 17:21). "Through the blood of these righteous ones and through the propitiation of their death the divine providence rescued Israel, which had been shamefully treated" (4 Macc. 17:22). The martyr Eleazar turns his eyes heavenward as his flesh is being burned from his bones, "You know, O God, that though I could have saved myself I am dying in these fiery torments for the sake of the Law. Be merciful to your people and let our punishment be a satisfaction on their behalf. Make my blood their purification and take my life as a ransom for theirs" (4 Macc. 6:27-29).

Nevertheless, the above wasn't quite the same as God sending his own son to earth and sacrificing Him to atone for the sins of humankind. To find precedents for the idea of Christ the Savior as presented in particular in the Gospels and the Book of Revelation, one, therefore, has to look at other examples. Harpur sees aspects of the savior theme in which a heavenly king descends into the dark lower world, "suffering dying, and rising again, before returning to his native upper world,"[6] as being an integral part of almost every religious faith the world over, with the account of Christ's life, His sayings, His miracles, as well as His death and resurrection as presented in the Gospels being most similar to the

Egyptian myths concerning the Egyptian gods Horus and Osiris, and in particular the former, whom Harpur sees as the "archetypal Pagan Christ."[7]

There are, no doubt, a great many similarities between the Egyptian gods Horus and Osiris and Christ as presented in the Bible. These can be found in comments attributed to these deities and to Christ, in the resurrection experience, and in particular in the different miracle works performed by Christ and also these deities. Unlike in the case of the Egyptian deities, however, the Bible, and in particular the Book of Revelation, ties Christ's death and resurrection into the end of time conflict between good and evil, with the triumph of good ushering in the final judgment, the banishment of evildoers to hell and the ascent of the followers of the true faiths to heaven and everlasting happiness. These beliefs have their origin, not in Egyptian mythology, but in Zoroastrianism.

As Zoroastrianism had such a significant influence on the view of salvation as presented in Scripture, in particular in the Book of Revelation, it may be of interest to explore a little further why and how Persian Zoroastrianism may have been absorbed into the Jewish faith. Before doing so, however, it is important to emphasize that there is little evidence that the Jews consciously adopted the religious beliefs of other peoples. Several influences would have militated against this. One was the Jewish belief that theirs was the most powerful and the only true God. This would have made it difficult for them to accept the religious beliefs of other peoples. This was reinforced by their view that they were a people apart, and even in Babylon they sought to keep themselves apart, in particular in the area of religious practices.

The Jews appear to have adopted certain beliefs of other peoples, not to replace their own, but to help them better sustain their own belief system. New ideas and beliefs, thereby, became weapons of defense, especially against beliefs of people who ruled them. This would have been encouraged in particular during the Second Temple period, or the period between Nehemiah's being sent to Judah by the Persian king (ca. 445 BC) and the time when Rome destroyed Herod's Temple and dispersed the Jewish inhabitants of Jerusalem (70 AD). With the conquest of Judah and the destruction of the Temple, the Jewish people had essentially lost their political independence. Many of them were dispersed or had fled. The population that remained was diluted with other peoples moving into the territory vacated. The possibility of Israel or Judah becoming a regional political or military power was slight to non-existent. Its political leaders were essentially appointees of foreign powers. At the same time, the Persians gave the Yahwist religious hierarchy control over the religious life of the people. Therefore, Judah was at core a theocracy, with its religious leaders assuring people's faithfulness to the Yahwist religion, while foreign governments held political and military power.

Prior to this, a major measurement used to determine the extent to which the community and its leaders had pleased their tribal deity was the extent to which he supported them militarily. This became impossible as the community was little able to wage war against other groups. At the same time, the community continued to hold the view that it had the most powerful deity. Also, it perceived itself as the community of light, with the correct faith, and perceived other people as having false gods who represented negative, darker forces. This would have made Zoroastrianism, with its focus on the conflict between the forces of light and darkness, with the eventual triumph of the forces of light over the forces of darkness, particularly attractive to them.

Here I must emphasize that the objective of this study is not to examine the Zoroastrian religion. Rather, my objective is to point to certain aspects of the Zoroastrian faith that appear to have been absorbed by both Judaism and Christianity, which influenced the manner in which salvation was sought in either of these religious traditions. I must emphasize, I am not arguing for a direct cause-effect relationship. I am saying that there are certain elements that were not at all or little present in the Jewish faith prior to Judah's coming under the control of the Persians and into contact with the Zoroastrian faith.

Similarities which the scholar Mary Boyce noticed between Zoroastrianism, Judaism and the later Christianity caused her to suggest that the latter two faiths were strongly influenced by the Persian faith of Zoroastrianism. At times she goes so far as to suggest that the Persians had a direct influence on Jewish and later Christian beliefs.[8] Barr, in turn, argues that the Persian influence on Judaism and the later Christianity did not come from the direct influence of Persian Zoroastrianism on the Jews. Rather,

From Earthly Event to Apocalyptic Vsion   105

the Persian Zoroastrian influence came to the Jews largely through the influence of the Greeks. He sees the Jews taking little interest in Zoroastrian thought. It was the Greeks, in particular Greek curiosity that caused them to explore Persian religious thought, and the Jews became aware of Persian religious thought as they became familiar with Greek culture. Rather than adopt Persian ideas to make them a part of their own faith, they used these ideas to counter Greek cultural expansionism. Thus, rather than absorb Persian thought, the Jews applied these concepts to defend their own religion during the Hellenistic domination of Palestine.[9]

Yamuachi, in turn, claims that scholars such as Boyce and Barr overestimated the influence of Zoroastrianism on Judaism and Christianity.[10] He sees their case being undercut by the necessity of our having to rely upon ninth century AD Pahlavi texts, which are our major sources for the eschatological views of Zoroastrianism.[11] Of course, in addition to an oral record, there had been earlier written accounts of Zoroaster's teachings. These were largely destroyed during the attacks launched by Alexander the Great against Zoroastrian religious leaders during the Greek conquest of Persia. Further destructions occurred during and following the Islamic conquest of Persia, when the major part of the population embraced the Islamic faith and, with it, sought to wipe out the remaining vestiges of their old faith.

The exact date of birth of Zoroaster is unknown. He is believed to have been born and active in Persia sometime between 1500 and 1000 BC. He preached monotheism in a land that followed an aboriginal polytheistic religion. Although at first persecuted for his religion, he eventually won the support of the king, and Zoroastrianism remained the state religion under various Persian rulers until the seventh century AD.

As already stated, Zoroaster saw the universe ruled by two main forces, one positive and the other negative. The force personified by Ahura Mazda worked for the good. All good emanated from Ahura Mazda and the spirits active on his behalf. Forces personified by Ahriman, the fiendish and destructive spirit, opposed him. These two forces, in conflict with each other, influenced the thoughts and behavior of people, causing them to do either good or evil. This would continue until the apocalyptic battle between the forces of Ahura Mazda and Ahriman.

The seed of Zoroaster was seen to play a central role in this transformation leading to the final battle between the forces of Ahura Mazda and Ahriman and those allied with him. With each virgin birth, an offspring of Zoroaster would work toward guiding people closer to Ahura Mazda and closer to righteousness, thereby leading humankind gradually closer to the good. Their efforts would lead to the final battle and the defeat of Ahriman, with a semi-divine Zoroaster leading the victorious onslaught over evil on behalf of Ahura Mazda. This would occur in the final days, the days preceding the final judgment, following which Ahriman and his followers would be cast down to hell, where they would remain until purified, when they would join the forces of good in heaven.

Of course, the idea of the end of days does not play itself out in quite the same way in Judaism as in Zoroastrianism. Thus, Zoroastrianism speaks of an end of time when both good and evil will be judged, when people all over the world who have done good and all the people who have done evil will be judged. One group will go to paradise, and the other will go to hell to be punished and purified before going to heaven. The prophets use a similar concept, in a different way. The end of time, the day of the Lord, will arrive when the righteous remnant of Israel shall be rewarded. It will not be the beginning of a new age, a new heaven and a new earth that Zoroastrianism speaks of. Rather, it will herald in the time when the Lord will at last reward the faithful remnant for having persevered in the faith. At that time, the heathens will acknowledge the glory of the Lord. The Jews will not be a subject people but will rule over others. This suggests that Jewish religious leaders did not directly absorb Zoroastrian beliefs but drew on them to bolster their own system of beliefs.

The influence of Zoroastrianism on the Jewish faith is also evident in another important way. Prior to their expulsion to Babylon, the Israelite God was very much involved with the fate of the Israelites in the Holy Land. In many ways, He acted like a tribal god of ancient times. However, following the Babylonian exile, He became much more universal in nature. In a sense, He was presented in a much broader perspective, and was frequently characterized by virtues that in Zoroastrianism are attributed to Ahura Mazda. He still remained in many ways a tribal god. At the same time, He became a defender of many of the virtues of social justice that are given much more emphasis in Zoroastrianism than they are in early Judaism. That is not to say that the Israelite deity did not exhibit some of these characteristics before. It was a matter of focus, with social ills and the community's failure to live up to expectations in this area being given much more emphasis after the return from Babylon than had been the case before.

The influence of Zoroastrianism on Judaism is evident in particular in what Cohn sees as novel views introduced into Judaism in the Book of Daniel: the concepts of the resurrection, eternal life, and reward and punishment after death. Of course, elements of these ideas had been present in Judaism and other faiths as well. Thus, the idea that God or the gods can awaken people from the dead is not unique to Zoroastrianism. In Egyptian mythology, the god Horus performed a great miracle at Anu, where he raised his father, Osiris, from the dead, calling unto him in the cave to "rise and come forth."[12] The Babylonians saw their god Marduk restoring life from the grave.[13] Components of the idea of resurrection were also present in biblical thought from earliest times. That God can revive the dead is one of His praises: "I kill and I make alive; I wound and I heal" (Deut. 32:39). Also, "The Lord kills and makes alive; He brings down to the grave and brings up" (I Sam. 2:6). God's power to destroy human beings and return them to life is also exhibited through the acts of Elijah and Elisha (I Kings 17: 17 ff.; II Kings 4: 18ff.).

In poetry, intense misery, severe sickness and extreme peril are identified as death-like states, with the victim descending into Sheol, the (nethermost) pit, or the depths of the sea (Psalms 30:3; 71:20; 88: 4-7; 143:3). The Lord's rescue from these states is identified as "restoring to life" (Psalms 30:3; 71:20; 143:11; Isaiah 38: 17ff.), "redemption from the pit," and the "restoration to youth" (Psalms 103: 4-5; Job 33: 24-30). The victim is cut off or feels himself to be cut off and wishes to be restored to "the land(s) of the living" (Isaiah 38:11; 53:8; Psalms 27:13; 116:9; Job 28:13).

However, the idea of resurrection as expressed in the Book of Daniel (12:2-3) is in many ways quite different from any of the above. Thus, Daniel writes that in a future time of great trouble, deliverance will come during which "many of those who sleep in the dust of the earth shall awake, some to everlasting life, some to shame and everlasting contempt. Those who are wise shall shine like the brightness of the firmament; and those who turn many to righteousness like the stars forever and ever" (Daniel 12: 2-3). That is to say, reward and punishment will be meted out after death, with both those who walk in the ways of the Lord and those who leave the faith obtaining their just deserts.

This idea of reward and punishment has much more in common with Zoroastrianism than with earlier similar concepts in Scripture. The resurrection of the dead in preparation for being punished or rewarded for their deeds on earth is an integral part of Zoroastrianism. At the same time, Zoroastrianism speaks of those who follow in the ways of Ahura Mazda being rewarded with eternal life. Those doing wrong will be punished and go to hell. Daniel, on the other hand, speaks essentially of Jews who remain faithful to the true faith being rewarded with eternal life. Rather than going to heaven, however, they will have eternal life on earth where they will live forever and rule over the heathens. But those who fall away from the Lord will be eternally punished.

The influence of Zoroastrianism appears to be much greater in Christianity than in traditional Judaism. This is evident in several areas. The Israelites had essentially two, not necessarily exclusive, views of salvation. People were rewarded as individuals as well as a collectivity. Thus, the Bible speaks of Abraham being rewarded for his faithfulness to God. He is rewarded by founding a people. The Book of Job focuses on God punishing or rewarding individual behavior, with reward or punishment being in the temporal sphere, with God giving or taking such things as riches or large families. While the Old Testament pays attention to rewards to the individual, the focus tends to be on rewards to the collectivity and the salvation of the collectivity. Thus, in the Book of Joshua, the entire community is punished when Achan the son of Carmi and others retained goods that had been designated for the Lord. It is rewarded again through victories over the idolaters when Achan the son of Carmi is stoned for these transgressions (7 Joshua: 1-16). In the Book of Daniel, the individual who remains true to the faith is rewarded. However, the reward accrues to the tribal collectivity, with all those who remain faithful being given eternal life and rule over the Gentiles.

The view of salvation enunciated by Christ is in many ways different from the above. This is evident in several areas. Thus, the salvation that Christ speaks of, for example in his parable of the rich and the poor man, involves the salvation strictly of the individual. Thus, the rich man goes to hell because of his deeds. The poor man goes to heaven, it is assumed because he has suffered on earth and has acted correctly. In this case, it is the individual standing before God who is judged worthy of heaven or hell. Punishment or reward accrues to him solely rather than to a tribal remnant as they do in the Book of Daniel. Furthermore, punishment is handed out in terms of going to heaven or going to hell. This vision has little to do with reward and punishment as described in traditional Judaism, but rather presents to us the basic criteria through which salvation is attained in the Zoroastrian religion.

There are also other aspects of the Christian belief system that appear to have been strongly influenced by ideas and concepts foreign to traditional Judaism. This is evident, for example, in the idea of Christ as savior. Of course, the idea of savior arises out of a particular Israelite tradition. Generally he is seen as someone who, with the support of God, helps the community deal with a particularly difficult situation. Christ as savior, however, brings a new message, a message directed toward letting people know how they may gain eternal rewards after death and escape eternal punishment. This message has more in common with Zoroastrianism than with traditional Judaism.

At the same time, arguments for Christ's divinity usually center on his crucifixion and resurrection leading to some end of time period when all of humankind will be judged and be found worthy of either heaven or hell. The issue of resurrection didn't even concern earlier Israelites and became a matter of debate among Israelites only after their contact with the Persians, when the belief in resurrection was accepted by part of the community, the Pharisees, and rejected by others, the Sadducees.

Of course, early Christians radically altered both the Jewish and Zoroastrian idea of resurrection when they argued that it was proof of Christ's divinity. Both Zoroastrianism and Judaism of the Second Temple period speak of the resurrection of all dead humans at the end of time. Neither of them suggests that resurrection is proof of divinity. In fact, logically speaking, it is hard to see in Christ's resurrection a proof of His divine nature when all of humankind will eventually be resurrected. The association made between Christ's resurrection and His divine nature must therefore be seen as a reinterpretation of commonly accepted ideas of resurrection of the time, embarked upon by Christians to explain their experiences with their leader following His crucifixion.

Aspects of Christ's birth as it is presented to us in Scripture show the influence of Zoroastrianism. Like the Zoroastrian saviors, Christ was born of a virgin. No other Israelite savior was born of a virgin. Magis, who were priests of the Zoroastrian faith, came to visit Christ. Both heaven and earth co-operated in bringing about the birth of Christ. This would also be the case in particular of the last reincarnated Zoroastrian savior. As a representative of Ahura Mazda, his birth would result in the final confrontation between the forces of Ahura Mazda and those of Ahriman, which would lead to the conquest of evil and to the reconciliation between humanity and the forces of the good.

In many ways, the salvation Christ promised grew out of this religious belief system rather than out of traditional Judaism. As did Zoroaster, Christ spoke of individual salvation rather than the collective salvation promised by traditional Judaism. Christ focused on choice that had consequences for the individual in the hereafter. While this also came into focus after the Israelite contact with the Persian world after their expulsion to Babylonia, traditional Judaism concentrates on rewards in the temporal sphere, that is, reward in this world rather than in heaven. Christ spoke of the choice being between going to heaven or going to hell in the afterlife. The heaven and the hell that Christ described, and the choices people have relating to either, have much more in common with Zoroastrianism than with the traditional Jewish faith.

The end of the world and the creation of a new type of universal order prophesied in the Book of Revelation is an integral part of Zoroastrianism. As already mentioned, in particular in reference to Noah's flood, the Bible speaks of God's regretting having created man because of his moral corruptness. God did not destroy man on this occasion because of the righteousness of one man. However, the idea of time as we know it ending with righteousness triumphing over unrighteousness, whose agents are sent to hell, is pure Zoroastrianism. The idea of looking at life as essentially a preparation for the judgment and reward and punishment in the afterlife doesn't appear in the tradition of the Israelites until they come into contact with the Persians. In this respect, the influence of other faiths, in particular of Zoroastrianism, played an integral role in helping to transform the Jewish faith, helping to prepare the way from the Holy Land as described in the Book of Joshua to the New Jerusalem as described in the Book of Revelation.

However, one must emphasize that there is little evidence that these changes resulted from the direct absorption of Zoroastrianism by Judaism. Yet, once Jewish religious leaders absorbed certain ideas in Zoroastrianism to help them explain their circumstances to themselves, these ideas then also came to transform the Jewish faith. In fact, one might well argue that the basic tenets of the Christian schism of the Jewish faith are in essence Zoroastrian rather than Jewish. Thus, the idea of a person choosing and then being rewarded with heaven or hell are central to both Christianity and Zoroastrianism. It is not central to traditional Judaism. The end-of-time depiction, the resurrection, and the afterlife as described in the Book of Revelation are in many ways an elaboration of end-of-time views as first presented in the Zoroastrian religion. Of course, the idea of Christ the divine Savior, grew out of the experiences of His followers following His crucifixion. At the same time, it evolved from the Israelite tradition. That is, it evolved from the Israelite hope for a savior.

In fact, in many ways Christ may be seen as a Zoroastrian savior with a Jewish pedigree. Of course, as Akenson reiterates again and again,[14] it was largely the ambiguous nature of biblical prophecy that allowed followers of Christ to identify Him as the long-awaited Messiah of Israel.[15] This connection, as Akenson emphasizes, often had more to do with the Christian effort to use and expand upon metaphorical prophetic writings in the biblical text than it did with readily discernible links between Christ the Son of God, Savior of humankind, and Christ the long-awaited Messiah who would satisfy Israel's aspirations.[16]

Although there is no clear connection between Christ the Savior and the Jewish Messiah, in another way Christ's message is an integral part of the tradition toward which Second Temple Judaism was evolving. This is evident when one focuses, not on the Christ the sacrificial Lamb offered up to save humanity from the fires of hell, but on Christ's teachings. For both Christ and other Jews of the Second Temple period, moral behavior was an important means of gaining God's support. Christ, however, went an extra step, minimizing ritual and stressing the importance of thought and action through which to gain God's blessings. Jews as a group tended to be divided regarding blessings accruing to the individual in the afterlife. At the same time, they expected certain benefits to be bestowed upon the collectivity as a reward for correct behavior. Christ, however, did not see rewards accruing to any collectivity as a result of moral behavior by the individual. The individual was the sole beneficiary of his moral behavior. He also would bear the punishment resulting from immoral behavior. Reward and punishment would come in the afterlife, following the resurrection and judgment. This view of salvation, at its core, is probably the most complete expression of the transformative effect Zoroastrianism had on the Jewish faith.

Conclusion

Persistent Patterns and Change

A. Continuity

From the Holy Land to the New Jerusalem and the Biblical View of Man and God

The evolution from the hopes of utopia in the Holy Land to the visions of utopia in the New Jerusalem may be seen as having its basis, ultimately, in a particular view of humanity and of God and the relationship between them. This relationship was structured largely by the reward and punishment nature of God's interaction with humankind.

The view of God as presented in the Bible tends to be fairly consistent. He is seen as universal, all-powerful. He had entered into a special relationship with the Israelites and had chosen them as His people. He was their deity and was active on their behalf. In particular, He rewarded them when they did those things that He demanded of them. If He did not act in their favour, He did so largely because they or a member (usually an important member) of their community had erred in some way so as to earn His punishment. This reward and punishment pattern tends to be fairly consistent and as a consequence had a strong influence on the evolution of the biblical message.

The view of the human race is also fairly consistent. Integral to this view is the belief that humanity in its fallen state is worthy of destruction and punishment. That is why the Israelites could slaughter the idolaters with impunity. That is why the slain Lamb as presented in Revelation can send all those who do not accept his message of grace to eternal damnation.

The Primacy of Morality and Belief

The basic biblical message is that human beings are acceptable only if they subject themselves to the laws of God. In fact, they are not merely acceptable; they are worthy of special blessings and even of eternal bliss. Otherwise, they are worthy of being killed, suppressed, and even eternally punished.

Thus, in the case of the Book of Joshua, the idolaters are destroyed so that the Israelites can better follow the regulations that will make them pleasing unto God and win His rewards. In the Book of Daniel, the Jews who keep the faith are granted eternal life and domination over the Gentiles while those who lose the faith are condemned to eternal suffering.

Morality and faith take on an even greater significance in the case of the Book of Revelation. Here, the entire universe is transformed, with the world as we know it being destroyed, so that the believers in a certain faith can enjoy eternal blessedness and the non-believers punished. Plant life, animal life, the order of the universe as we know it, become nothing compared to enforcing a certain belief and certain behavioral patterns.

The Central Role of the Holocaust in Salvation and the Realization of Utopia

In the case of the founding of the Holy Land, the destruction of the idolaters is an integral part of founding a place where the people of Israel can hope to attain the Paradise-like existence promised unto them by their deity. In the case of the realization of the New Jerusalem, the destruction of non-believers and their removal to hell is an integral part of establishing an abode where the blessed of the Lord can exist in eternal bliss. Hell, which in Zoroastrianism was in many respects a process of purification, in the Christian transformation becomes a means of satisfying the righteous anger of the Lord toward non-believers, who by their very nature are depicted as evil, in opposition to the righteous who enter heaven. The sacrifice of one group, in this context, becomes an integral part of a religious ritual in which one segment of humanity is sacrificed so as to permit another to maximize the blessings it hopes to realize from the deity in control of the universe and the destiny of humankind.

B. Change

While the above outlooks remained constant, others altered. Thus, the belief system and how it expressed itself changed. This may be seen in:

The Nature of God's Actions

At first, God interacted closely with His chosen, carrying out His and their goals through them. Increasingly, God became ever more distant. Eventually, He is described as acting, not through His chosen on earth but through the Son of Man, or through His own Son to combat the forces of evil in the universe and thereby prepare the way for salvation for the chosen and the way to condemnation for the followers of evil.

Changes in the Nature of Rewards and of Punishment

At first, disbelievers might be enslaved or killed so as to help prepare the next best thing to Paradise on earth for the elect. Finally, those worthy of salvation are promised eternal blessedness after the resurrection, while non-believers, who also are seen as evil, are designated for eternal punishment in hell following the final resurrection.

Changes in how Time is Viewed

In the Book of Joshua, the action takes place in time as we know it. In the Book of Revelation, reward and punishment are seen to take place after death. Reward and punishment are seen to be forever rather than for the duration of any specific time period.

A Change in Focus

Up to the conquest and the destruction of Jerusalem by the Babylonians, the biblical record focuses on the state of Israel as a given political and social unit. After the destruction, the focus is increasingly on some future salvation to be gained by those Hebrews who maintain the faith. Choices made by each individual community member will determine whether he or she will belong among the elect. The individual comes into focus even more succinctly in Christ's message, where each individual, regardless of ethnic origin, determines, on the basis of the choices made, whether he or she is destined for heaven or hell.

Changes in the Nature of War and Conquest

When the Israelites took over what came to be called the Holy Land, they felt themselves to be strong enough, with their deity's help, to destroy the ancient inhabitants of the land. People were involved in warfare as we know it. At the same time, victory was seen as ensuing from their ability to recruit their deity to fight on their behalf.

After the Babylonian conquest in 587 BC, the emphasis was not on people gaining their ends through warfare with the support of their deity. The focus was on God attaining the goals of the Israelites among other people without their having to resort to the sword. God himself would attain these, if believers did all those things God demanded of them. That is, God would fight on their behalf and attain for them the goals to which they aspired.

Christ the Man as Described by the Apostles is Transformed into a Zoroastrian-type Savior

Although this doesn't apply to the biblical text as a whole, it is nevertheless important to point out how John's image of the Zoroastrian-like savior in the Book of Revelation transformed the image of Christ as he is presented in the Gospels. Major differences are evident in several areas. Before discussing these, it is important to point out that there is some difference of opinion regarding the nature of Christ as he is presented to us in the Gospels. Looking at these, Marcus Borg differentiates between what he calls Jesus seen through "Christian doctrinal lens," and the "historical" Jesus. To illustrate the difference, Borg examines Jesus as he is presented in the Book of Mark and in a written collection of the teachings of Jesus that scholars call "Q." With the gospel of Mark written about 70 AD and "Q" written earlier, the two are seen as the basis on which later synoptic gospels, Matthew and Luke, were written. Borg argues that earlier writings, such as the gospel of Mark and the "Q" document show Christ as having been essentially a Jewish mystic centred on God. Later writings, those presenting Christ as divine, were a product largely of attempts by Christ's followers to comprehend his crucifixion and resurrection.[1]

No matter whether one looks at Christ as a Jewish mystic or as the Son of God, Christ, as presented to us by the Apostles is radically different from the view of him we receive from John's Book of Revelation. In many respects, except for the miracles he performed, writings attributed to the Apostles present Christ as not that different from other men. That is, he suffered many of the same trials and tribulations. The main difference between him and others was the manner in which he overcame them. At the same time, Christ suggested codes of behaviour according to which people should conduct their life. Thus, rather than resorting to the sword to fight aggression, he counselled turning the other cheek. He counselled forgiveness rather than revenge, and in many ways suggested that faith and the love of God expressed itself in a practical manner through service to humankind.

Insofar as Christ spoke of a superhuman being, he spoke of the Son of Man, who at the end of time as we know it, will judge the wicked and the good, with the wicked being punished and the good enjoying the blessings of the kingdom of God. This judgement will focus on each individual being punished or rewarded according to his thoughts and behaviour. In this regard, Christ stressed in particular the relationship between belief and one's treatment of one's fellow man. Thus, the Son of Man will separate the righteous from the unrighteous, not so much according to whether or not they ascribed to a particular belief system, but rather according to the degree to which they adhered to the will of the Father. The righteous, who cared for their fellow beings, in particular the poor and the unfortunate, would be rewarded with the blessings of the Kingdom of God. The unrighteous, who focused on aggrandizing themselves and satisfying their own selfish needs, would be punished.

John, on the other hand, in the Book of Revelation, identified Christ the slain Lamb as the Son of Man. This Son of Man will be much more aggressive than the Son of Man of whom Christ spoke. In fact, John didn't focus at all on the role of the Son of Man as a judge evaluating individual behaviour. Rather, the arrival of

John's Son of Man will be accompanied by great battles in which Christ the Lamb will fight the Anti-Christ on behalf of the community of the saved. In this process, the world as we know it will be destroyed. Satan will be vanquished and sent to hell with all evildoers, while people with the correct faith will go to heaven.

In all this, John naturally assumed that in each case correct faith results in correct action and not having the true faith would cause people to indulge in all those acts God condemns. By concentrating on the collectivity and on war as a means of salvation, John in many ways altered Christ's message of salvation. It is no longer basically a message directed to individuals, encouraging them to do those things that would help them attain the Kingdom of God. Rather, John concentrated on a universal war that will bring about the destruction of the old universal order and the establishment of a new universal order. The broader outline of this struggle is very similar to that presented to us in the establishment of the Holy Land: eliminating a negatively typed community becomes an integral part of creating an ideal environment for the elect. However, the community of the elect in this case is a community of believers rather than essentially a tribal community. Members thereof are promised heaven rather than the next best thing to Paradise. The enemies of the elect, in turn, are sent to hell rather than killed.

At the same time, the results of the end-of-time battles John described are quite different from those that led to the establishment of the Holy Land. Members of the new group of elect will not find themselves threatened with punishment should they deviate from the way of the Lord. In fact, it will be impossible for them to do so. The evil one who led humans into sin will be bound and punished forever, along with his followers. The elect, on the other hand, will enjoy eternal blessedness.

The Ascent from the Holy Land to the New Jerusalem as an Attempt to Understand the Workings of an All-powerful God

The change from salvation being sought in the temporal sphere to the pursuit of salvation in the eternal sphere may be seen as evolving from the endeavour by the Israelite religious leadership to sustain their belief in an all powerful deity.

At the time of the founding of Israel, God promised His chosen the next best thing to Paradise. In particular, He did not promise that they would experience subjugation in their own land. The non-fulfilment of God's promise was explained in several ways. One way in which this was done was to blame the people themselves; God had not granted them victory over their enemies because they had sinned. Of course, it is not within the scope of this work to examine the sins of the people of Israel to determine whether their behaviour was worthy of the punishments they had to suffer because of their transgressions. It is enough to say that the priesthood when accounting for the numerous defeats the Israelites had to undergo, in particular following the breakup of the united monarchy, was to attribute them to sin. This was the case in the Books of Kings, for example, where the different royal leaders were seen as having failed to carry out the rituals demanded of them, failed to remain true to the worship of the only one true God, and thus were punished by being defeated by their enemies.

Following the destruction of Jerusalem and the expulsion of many of its citizens to Babylon, the Book of Isaiah attributed this punishment to the multitude of sins the people had committed. There wasn't one area in God's laws where the people hadn't transgressed, thereby justifying God's punishment. At the same time, the return of the small remnant under Cyrus II, after he conquered Babylon, was used to argue that, with this, God had given his people another chance. God could have totally destroyed them had He chosen to do so, but He had not done so because He wanted to give them another opportunity to redeem themselves.

This interpretation of the fate of the Israelites helped to keep alive the faith in an all-powerful God in several ways. It laid the defeats, not at the feet of God, but at the feet of the people who had failed to live up to what their God demanded of them; therefore the defeats and resulting treatment were justified. At the same time, in particular when the people were blamed, there were so many areas of fault or so many people included under this wide umbrella of possible transgressors that it would have been impossible to argue against such blanket accusations. Also, the accusations were part of a call to try harder to be faithful, to carry out the commandments, and then be rewarded. This interpretation did two things: it justified the punishment, and it offered the hope of eventually gaining God's rewards.

Furthermore, the possibility of gaining rewards was moved further and further into the future. At the time of Joshua, God's action was described as taking place in the here and now. Thus, Yahweh was described as advising Joshua on how to carry out the conquest. God also took an active role in the conquest. In the case of David, God often advised on how best to pursue a certain battle plan. Even in the case of the different kings who had strayed from the ways of the Lord, He was involved in their fate in the here and now. He was involved, for example, in miracles carried out by prophets such as Elijah and Elisha so as to help persuade the king of the authenticity and power of God. He was involved in using defeat to punish the different kings for their evil ways.

Soon after the destruction of Jerusalem and the return of the remnant, however, there is a significant alteration in the way God's actions were interpreted. God's decisive act on behalf of His people to reward them for their faithfulness was increasingly described as taking place, not in the here and now, but in some end-of-time framework, in the end of days. It is not certain as to when this would be. At the same time, the nature of God's acting on behalf of His people altered. In fact, His people's main role in God's plan of salvation was for them to keep the faith and follow the commandments. Then God would act on their behalf. God would not use them as a means of conquering the Gentiles as He had done in the case of the idolaters. God himself would create situations where other nations would recognize His power and glory, and the Temple in Jerusalem would become a house of prayer for all peoples. At the same time, God would place the Israelites in a position where they would not be dominated but would have dominance over other peoples, in particular those who in the past showed enmity toward them.

This theme is developed further in the Book of Daniel, where the reward is also placed in an end-of-time context. Here it is stated even more clearly that power will be the reward for faithfulness. God, acting through the vaguely conceptualized Son of Man, conducts the battle. The main demand is that the Jews do not discard the true faith. Jews who retained their faith in Yahweh,

Conclusion 121

including those who are to be resurrected, would be granted eternal life. Those who did not keep the faith would be subjected to eternal punishment. The faithful remnant, rather than being ruled by the Gentiles, would have power over them.

Of course, both Isaiah and the Book of Daniel have to be read in context. The segment of the Book of Isaiah dealing with the destruction of Jerusalem and the expulsion of Jews to Babylon are intended not merely to describe these events. They also serve to persuade as many of the exiles as possible to return from Babylon and not give up on the collective dream that Israel and the temple in Jerusalem represented. The Book of Daniel was written when Antiochus IV was seeking to impose emperor worship on the Jews and when a great many Jews were becoming Hellenised and falling away from the faith. It was written to persuade people to remain true to the traditional faith because the rewards it promised were much greater than those people might gain by giving up the faith and becoming fully Hellenised.

To help preserve the faith that the Jewish people were God's special beloved, their religious leaders increasingly pointed, not to what God did in the here and now, but to what God would bestow upon them if they retained the faith. They drew not only on their traditional beliefs but also, in particular, on Zoroastrianism to help sustain the faith. This eventually led to a transformation of beliefs. This transformative process occurred gradually, being somewhat evident in the Book of Isaiah, increasingly evident in the Book of Daniel, and still more evident in Christ's message. In fact, although Christ the Savior evolved from the Hebrew messianic tradition, Christ's message of salvation parted in radical ways from that of traditional Judaism.

The Book of Revelation combines the traditional with the Christian view of salvation. Thus, John sees both Jews who remain true to the faith and devoted to its practices, as well as the followers of Christ, going to heaven at the end of time. It describes how this salvation will come about. At the same time, the Book carries to a conclusion the Israelite savior tradition. However, it transforms this tradition. The savior, rather than offering salvation essentially for the Jews, opens the possibility of salvation for the Gentiles on an equal basis with the Jews. That is, both Jews who remained true to the faith and Gentiles who accepted Christ as their savior would inherit and live in bliss in heaven and the New Jerusalem. Others would go to eternal perdition.

Two Visions of Salvation

The Movement from the Holy Land to the New Jerusalem as Part of God's Plan of Salvation for Humanity

The biblical record leading from the Holy Land to the New Jerusalem presents essentially two visions of salvation. Thus, the movement may be seen as part of God's plan of salvation. In particular Evangelical Christians hold this interpretation, seeing God as using the people of Israel to bring Christ into the world to offer salvation to all of humankind. In this context, the first holocaust and the prophesied last holocaust may be viewed as part of a plan whereby God promises ultimate salvation to those who choose Christ as their savior.

The main message in this context is that humans had started out as perfect. Through the fall, humankind turned away from the Lord and fell into sin. People have free will; they may act as God wants them to act or according to their lower, sinful nature. At the end of time, all people will be judged according to their behaviour, with those who acted in a manner pleasing unto the Lord going to heaven and those who did not do so going to hell. The Bible explains how and why God brought Christ into the world through the Israelites to impart this message to everyone. At the same time, in particular in the Book of Revelation, it presents a scenario of how the end-of-time events that will bring salvation to believers and condemnation to non-believers will unfold.

Salvation through God Satisfying the Power Needs of a Tribal Collectivity

The movement from the Holy Land to the New Jerusalem may also be seen as evolving from the belief of God being active primarily in the service of a tribal collectivity. Although at the time of the conquest of Palestine God promised to provide His people with the next best thing to Paradise, if they remained faithful to Him, there is little mention of this promise in most of the Bible.

Rather, as one follows God's relationship with His chosen through the Bible, the focus is on the deity's role in serving in particular the power needs of His followers. Thus, God participated in destroying the idolaters. God's role in serving the power needs of His people is also evident at the time when a monarch ruled Israel, when God in many ways acted as a war god, bringing victory to the Hebrews if they walked in His ways and bringing them defeat when they displeased Him. In the Book of Isaiah, His service in the interest of power continues, and we are told that God will eventually reward the blessed remnant that choose to walk in His ways by granting them dominance over the Gentiles. The same promise is made to Jews in the Book of Daniel, where Jews who remain true to the faith are to be given, not only dominance over the Gentiles, but also eternal life.

In all these cases, acting according to God's will is connected to the promise of power. There is an intricate relationship between doing the right thing and winning the favour of the deity. This favour invariably expresses itself through the granting of power, be this power for the Israelites to control their own destiny, or power for the Jewish people who remain true to the faith to dominate other peoples.

Of course, the Bible also insinuates that there is a relationship between the Jewish people attaining power and the rule of God's justice. This appears to be true in particular as far as the Israelites or the Judeans are concerned. The message is less clear with respect to other peoples. Thus, idolaters who were not killed by the Israelites were enslaved, with Solomon enslaving the descendants of the original inhabitants of the land who had not been destroyed. The Book of Isaiah speaks of some future time when justice will reign, where the lamb and the lion shall feed together, but in the same breath, it mentions that those people who do not bow down to the Israelites will be crushed and even obliterated. This suggests that the justice to be administered through the attainment of power by God's chosen is rather ambiguous for those who do not count among the elect.

Faith, the Human Experience, and the Evolution of Christianity from Judaism

Objectively looked at, the biblical record showing the movement from the Holy Land to the New Jerusalem can provide important insights into the relationship between history, religious belief and reality, and the needs these fulfill for the human psyche. In this regard, several observations may be made. One is the importance of belief as an integrative factor in the human experience. History itself, as a record of our temporal experience, appears to do little in this regard for humans. Religious belief, however, transcends human limitations in time and space, expands beyond the temporal, and ties the personal and the larger historical event into the universal. The movement from the Holy Land to the New Jerusalem provides a good example of how this is done and how belief and history interact to sustain a religious belief system.

Thus, the establishment of the Holy Land was one of the earliest examples we have of the attempt to found a utopia-like society. Its basic purpose was to create in the world a type of existence that approximated that of Paradise as described in Genesis. The attempt to create this led to the destruction of the idolaters. This, in turn, served to establish a base where the Israelites could establish and perpetuate their religious beliefs. The success in creating this base through appeal to the group deity, in turn, gave efficacy to the conviction that the Israelite God was the most powerful of deities and that the Hebrews were His beloved people, chosen to enjoy His blessings.

Then came the test of sustaining the belief through time, in particular the belief that Yahweh, as a war god, was the most powerful of deities. After all, in this respect Yahweh was little more than one of the many war gods ancients believed in. Gods, rather than people, were seen to make war, with the deity granting victory or defeat. Defeat or victory was, therefore, a readily available means whereby the power of a deity could be judged. Of course, if judged solely on this basis, the Israelite religious system would have disappeared long ago.

However, it sustained itself. It did so essentially by leaving an out for the deity. It did so by blaming the people either as individuals or as a group for defeats. As well, the possibility of reward was moved from the present into the future. Furthermore, God's action was interpreted in increasingly abstract terms, where it could be little judged through the use of one's faculties, including one's ability to reason. That is, it became increasingly mythological in nature. This is especially evident in the Book of Daniel and then, at the extreme, in the Book of Revelation.

At the same time, rewards and the punishment for non-belief became much more extreme. With this, also, the choice as to who belongs to the elect increasingly moves from God to the individual doing the choosing. Thus, in the first part of the Bible, the idolaters, who did not count among the elect, were killed. The Israelites, God's chosen, on the other hand, were left to enjoy the fruits of the land. Later, in the Book of Daniel, Jews who have fallen away from the faith will face eternal punishment. Those who remain true to the faith, in turn, are promised eternal life and rule over the Gentiles. In the Book of Revelation, believers are promised heaven. Non-believers are condemned to eternal hell fire.

Within this framework, any criteria for judging the truth or falsehood of the belief system were lost. The main reason for this is that maintaining the belief was much more important than any objective evaluation. Thus, the conviction that Yahweh was the most powerful deity in the universe and that they were His beloved people whom He would reward in some special way was much more important to the Israelites than attempting to measure the efficacy of their belief system objectively. Arguments regarding reward and punishment, moving the action of their deity increasingly into the future and interpreting the action of the deity in increasingly abstract terms, were simply means of sustaining belief in the face of any reality that put it into question.

However, this isn't the full explanation. While an understanding of historical events may allow us to obtain insight into the human condition in the temporal sphere, it doesn't satisfy deeper needs, such as our need to find a secure, predictable niche in the world and the larger universe. Included in this, of course, is the need to explain life and death. This made sustaining the belief system more important than establishing objective criteria for evaluating it and then accepting or rejecting it on this basis.

The study also gives insight into how one belief system evolved from another, with the new system taking form because of the difficulty traditional Judaism had accepting important aspects of the schism to which it had given rise. One problem posed by the schism was the belief that Christ was the Son of God. Jews of Christ's time considered the very suggestion of anyone claiming to be the divine son of Yahweh as blasphemous. Of course, Christians saw both Christ's birth and resurrection as proof of His divine nature. The belief in resurrection, combined with reward and punishment, became part of the Jewish faith only after the Jews came into contact with Persian Zoroastrianism. Once accepted, however, the belief was transformed. Thus, in the Book of Daniel, we have faithful Jews being resurrected to enjoy eternal life and rule over the gentiles, while unfaithful Jews are resurrected to be punished. In Zoroastrianism, all people are resurrected. In Christianity, this idea is retained. At the same time, Christ's resurrection is viewed as proof of His divinity. For them, Christ's resurrection is seen as preparing the way for their own eventual resurrection. This belief, of course, was alien to traditional Judaism.

Christians, however, saw Christ and His message as part of the Jewish tradition, connecting Christ, in particular, with the Jewish hope for a savior. Of course, the hope of a messiah grew out of the failure rather than the success the Israelites and, later, the Jews had with their deity as a war god. If the experience had been a success there would not have been a need for a messiah or savior. This failure, however, was attributed to the failures of the believers. One can well argue, therefore, that Christianity evolved from the manner in which the Israelites and Jewish people sought to sustain the belief that they were the especially beloved people of an all-powerful deity fighting on their behalf in their power struggle with other people. To sustain this conviction, they absorbed basic tenets of another faith and altered these to suit their needs. This in turn led to the emergence of ideas traditional Judaism found unacceptable, leading to Christ's crucifixion, the persecution of His followers, and the eventual emergence of a new belief system.

From this perspective, both Judaism and Christianity offer insight into how a faith becomes linked to events. They illustrate how events are interpreted to justify the faith. In this respect, they move from the possibly verifiable to the mythological. They illustrate the basic needs in people to keep a faith alive. At the same

Conclusion

time, they show how beliefs evolve to the point where they no longer serve the needs or explain experiences of significant elements of a religious community and thereby spawn a schism that an existing religious community was unable to integrate. From this perspective, the movement from the Holy Land to the New Jerusalem, the movement from the first to the last holocaust, may be seen as illustrating how religions emerge, evolve, transform, and sustain themselves, and, at the same time, bring forth a new belief system.

Of course, this conclusion is merely descriptive. It is based on the record of events showing how certain Jewish beliefs altered under changing circumstances, leading eventually to Christianity. However, my analysis cannot answer the following questions. Was this process simply a matter of people using and altering manmade beliefs to meet their needs? Or, rather, was this process an integral part of God's larger plan to reveal himself to stubborn, recalcitrant human kind, forging different means to encourage people to evolve in a manner that will bring humanity closer to Him? Then again, perhaps this work describes neither of the above. Perhaps this work merely describes the endeavour by people to take possession of and make their very own the universal force of love that we call God. Perhaps a holocaust is a natural consequence of the attempt by a collectivity, no matter how defined, to restrict the blessings of utopia, the love of God, to themselves.

Notes

Introduction

[1] Martin H. Manser and Nigel D. Turton, *The Penguin Wordmaster Dictionary* (Harmondsworth, Middlesex: Penguin Books, 1987): 334. Also, Henry George Liddell and Robert Scott, comp., *A Greek-English Lexicon*, new (9th) edition (Oxford: Clarendon Press, 1961): 1217.

[2] Francois Chamoux, *The Civilization of Greece*, trans. W.S. Maguinnes (New York: Simon & Schuster, 1965) 228.

[3] Thus, Anderson describes the *hêrem*, or the ancient Israelite practice, as in the case of the idolaters, of destroying an entire group, as a "holocaust or sacrifice." Bernard Anderson, *Understanding the Old Testament* (Edgewood Cliffs, NJ: Prentice Hall, 1957) 129, 138.

[4] Christina Larner, "Crimen Exceptum? The Crime of Witchcraft in Europe," *Witch-Hunting in Early Modern Europe*, vol. 3, ed. Brian P. Levack (New York: Garland Publishing, 1992) 3: 80.

[5] Wasyl Hryshko, *The Ukrainian Holocaust of 1933*, ed. and trans. Marco Carynnyk (Toronto: Bahriany Foundation, 1983) 109; Robert Conquest, *The Great Terror: A Reassessment* (Edmonton: University of Alberta Press, 1990) 487.

[6] Stephen Katz, *The Holocaust in Historical Context. Vol. I: The Holocaust and Mass Death before the Modern Age* (New York: Oxford University Press, 1994) 28. Yehuda Bauer, *The Holocaust in Historical Perspective* (Seattle: University of Washington Press, 1978) 32.

[7] See, for example, Philip Davies, "What separates a Minimalist from a Maximalist? Not Much," *Biblical Archaeology Review*, vol. 26, no. 2 (March/April 2000): 26-27, 72-73.

[8] Gonzalo Baez-Camargo, *Archaeological Commentary on the Bible* (New York: Doubleday, 1984) 66.

[9] E.M. Good, "Joshua, Book of," *The Interpreter's Dictionary of the Bible: An Illustrated Encyclopedia*, ed. G.A. Buttrick (New York: Abingdon Press, 1962) 993. See also William G. Dever, "Archaeology and the Israelite 'Conquest,'" *The Anchor Bible Dictionary*, vol. 3, ed. David Noel Freedman et al. (New York: Doubleday, 1992) 556.

[10] Dever, "Archaeology and the Israelite 'Conquest'" 548.

[11] William F. Albright, *The Archaeology of Palestine*, rev. ed. (Harmondsworth: Penguin Books, 1956).

[12] Baez-Camargo 66.

[13] Peter C. Craigie, *The Old Testament: Its Background, Growth and Content* (Burlington, ON.: Welch Publishing, 1986) 101.

[14] Baez-Camargo 58 - 66.

[15] Dever, "Archaeology and the Israelite 'Conquest'" 545 - 558.

[16] William G. Dever, "Archaeology and the Emergence of Early Israel," *Archaeology and Biblical Interpretation*, ed. John R. Bartlett (London and New York: Routledge, 1997) 22-24, 47-48.

[17] Dever, "Archaeology and the Emergence of Early Israel" 47.

[18] Others one might mention include Philip R. Davies, *In Search of 'Ancient Israel'* (Sheffield: JSOT Press, 1992); Keith W. Whitelam, *The Invention of Ancient Israel: the Silencing of Palestinian History* (London: Routledge, 1996); Thomas L. Thompson, *Biblical Archaeology and the Myth of Israel* (New York: Basic Books, 1999); Philip Davies, "What separates a Minimalist from a Maximalist? Not Much," *Biblical Archaeology Review*, vol. 26, no. 2 (March/April 2000): 26-27, 72-73; Israel Finkelstein and Neil A. Silberman, *The Bible Unearthed* (New York, NY: The Free Press, 2001).

[19] The main thrust of Finkelstein's argument is that the predominant segment of the Hebrew Bible was committed to written form at the time of King Josiah (639-609 BC) of Judah and to a great extent reflects the time period as well as the interests of Judah and its Davidinian monarchy.

[20] Niditch sees the ban, or hêrem, as part of the biblical war text through which all human beings among the defeated are 'devoted to destruction.' See Susan Niditch, *War in the Hebrew Bible: A Study in the Ethics of Violence* (New York: Oxford University Press, 1993) 28.

[21] Finkelstein and Silberman, *The Bible Unearthed* 119.

[22] Finkelstein and Silberman, on pages 235 and 241, for example.

[23] Ken R. Dark, *Theoretical Archaeology* (Ithaca, NY: Cornell University Press, 1995).

[24] G. Boling et al., *Joshua: A New Translation with Notes and Commentary* (New York: Doubleday and Co., 1982) 77.

[25] Boling et al. 54-72.

[26] The record of events of a later date suggests that the endeavour to destroy the original inhabitants of Palestine continued on after Joshua. Thus, we read in Samuel that God commanded Saul to totally wipe out the Amelekites, to not spare them, but "kill both man and woman, infant and suckling, ox and sheep, camel and ass," for their opposition to Israel on the way to the Holy Land (1 Samuel 15, 2-3). After Saul defeated the Amalekites from Havelah as far as Shur, east of Egypt, he destroyed all the people with the edge of the sword. However, he saved Agog, the king, as well as the choicest livestock. Samuel criticized Saul for not

carrying out the Lord's command, for he was to "'utterly destroy the sinners', the Amalekites, and fight against them until they are consumed" (1 Samuel 15: 18). David also totally destroyed the original inhabitants he conquered who still remained in the land (the Girzites, Gesherites, Amalekites), while he was hiding from Saul and lived among the Philistines (1 Samuel 27: 8-12). It seems such destruction was directed only against the remnant of people who were left following the initial conquest. The Israelites followed a different pattern of warfare with later arrivals, such as the Philistines. In this case, either one group or the other sought to enslave its enemy. At the same time, the Israelites sought to drive the Philistines out of the Israelite cities the latter had conquered (See for example, 1 Samuel 4: 9-12, and 1 Samuel 7: 13-14). There is also little evidence that David killed people conquered as he expanded the territory held or controlled by the Israelites. Attitudes toward the original inhabitants also changed. Thus, we read that at the height of Israelite glory under Solomon, all the people "who were left of the Amorites, the Hittites, the Perizzites, the Hivites, and Jebusites, who were not of the people of Israel - their descendants who were left after them in the land, whom the people of Israel were unable to destroy utterly - these Solomon made a forced levy of slaves..." (1 Kings 9: 20-22).

The above suggests several things. It suggests that Joshua's attempt to wipe out the original inhabitants of biblical Palestine was not an isolated incident but part of a prolonged effort. It suggests that some of the people escaped each killing spree by the Israelites; with some surviving until, eventually, they or their descendants were enslaved.

[27] Craigie, *The Old Testament* 266-67. This interpretation is also shared by Baez-Camargo 58.

Chapter 1

[1] Yvon Garlan, *War in the Ancient World: A Social History*, trans. Janet Lloyd (New York: W.W. Norton, 1975) 71. Also see T. Jacobsen, "Sumer," *The Encyclopedia of Ancient Civilizations*, ed. Arthur Cotterell (London: Macmillan, 1983) 79.

[2] Gerd Lüdemann, *The Unholy in Holy Scripture: The Dark Side of the Bible*, trans. John Bowden (Louisville, Kentucky: Westminster John Knox Press, 1997) 45. For the Israelites, the destruction was part of establishing a territory where they would be able to create an environment in which they would be able to worship their God without fear of contamination by other people, and through this ensure for themselves a Paradise-like existence. The Moabites, who according to the biblical record were the descendants of Abraham's nephew Lot, viewed the ban, or the total

destruction of the inhabitants of a locale that was conquered, strictly as a sacrifice to their deity.

³ Lüdemann 45-46.

⁴ O.R.Gurney, "The Hittites." *Encyclopedia of Ancient Civilizations*, ed. Arthur Cotterell (London: Macmillan, 1983) 115. See also Johannes Lehmann, *The Hittites: People of a Thousand Gods*, trans. J. Maxwell Brownjohn (New York: Viking Press, 1977) 266-267.

⁵ A.K. Grayson,"Assyria." *Encyclopedia of Ancient Civilizations*, ed.Arthur Cotterell (London:Macmillan, 1983) 106.

⁶ Thucydides, *The Poloponnesian War*, trans. Rex Warner (London: Cassell, 1962) 360.

⁷ Fustel De Coulanges, *The Ancient City: A Study on Religion, Laws, and Institutions of Greece and Rome* (Garden City, NY: Doubleday, 1956) 207.

⁸ B.H. Warmington, *Carthage* (London: Robert Hale Ltd., 1980) 124-127, 196-209.

⁹ It was this promise that also makes the destruction in the founding of the Holy Land not only quite different from destructions carried out by other groups in ancient times, but also similar to later mass destructions that came to be identified as holocausts. Thus, there is little evidence that Babylonians or Assyrians offered their own people an ideal environment through their conquests. However, the Israelites did, as also did the Nazis and the communists. The Nazis offered their own group ideal conditions under which to survive in the dog-eat-dog world of social Darwinism. The communists offered the proletariat their particular version of the communist utopia. The Israelites, in turn, offered their own particular group the next best thing to Paradise in this world. Of course, they would not live under the blessed conditions in which Adam and Eve found themselves. However, they would enjoy good health, well-being and abundance. Illness would be the lot of their enemies. In fact, they would live a life more blessed than any other people on earth. At the same time, to keep God's blessings flowing toward them, they had to destroy the idolaters so that these would not entice them to deviate from the ways of the Lord and, as a result, be punished.

In this context, the destruction of the idolaters illustrates dynamics scholars such as Stephen Katz or Yehuda Bauer later identified as what they saw as the unique characteristics of the destruction of European Jewry, or THE HOLOCAUST. Thus, Steven Katz argues that the Nazi destruction of European Jewry is "phenomenologically unique," basing his view on the claim that never prior to this has a state, "as a matter of intent and principle and actualizing policy," undertaken to destroy every member of a specific group. He therefore sees the term "holocaust" properly applying only to this genocide. A similar argument is put forward by Yehuda Bauer, who uses the term "holocaust" to differentiate between

Nazi aims for the Jews and their aims for other nationalities, such as the Czechs, Poles, or Gypsies. Of these groups, only the Jews were to be totally destroyed. He sees the main feature of the holocaust as being the focus on the total destruction of the target group, with the Nazi case, in his view, being the first time in history that a sentence of death has been pronounced on anyone guilty of having been born of certain parents. See Stephen Katz, *The Holocaust in Historical Context. Vol. I: The Holocaust and Mass Death before the Modern Age* (New York: Oxford University Press, 1994) 28; Yehuda Bauer, *The Holocaust in Historical Perspective* 32.

Chapter 2

[1] See, for example, Theodore Olson, *Millennialism, Utopianism, and Progress* (Toronto: University of Toronto Press. 1982) 73.

[2] John W. Marshall, *Parables of War: Reading John's Jewish Apocalypse* (Kitchener, ON: Wilfrid Laurier University Press, 2001) 55-77, 89.

[3] Marshall 140.

[4] Norman Rufus Colin Cohn, "Biblical Origins of the Apocalyptic Tradition," *The Apocalypse and the Shape of Things to Come*, ed. Frances Carey (Toronto: University of Toronto Press, 1999) 35.

Chapter 4

[1] Georges Roux, *Ancient Iraq*, second edition (Harmondsworth, Middlesex: Penguin Books Ltd., 1980) 275.

[2] Roux 286.

[3] Roux 287.

[4] Roux 284.

[5] Roux 345.

[6] Roux 345.

[7] Roux 346.

[8] Roux 347.

[9] Morris Jastrow, *The Civilization of Babylonia and Assyria: Its Remains, Language, History, Religion, Commerce, Law, Art, and Literature*. First publ. 1915. Reissued 1971 (New York, NY: Benjamin Blom, 1971) 237-238. Jastrow describes the relationship among the Assyrian gods, punishment, and sin. War was undertaken in the name of the gods, and victory was seen as being granted by the gods. Defeat was interpreted as a punishment for having displeased the gods.

[10] Roux 348.

[11] Roux 353.

[12] Roux 354.

[13] A. Olmstead, *History of the Persian Empire* (Chicago: The University of Chicago Press, 1948) 50-51.

[14] Roux 358.
[15] Roux 358.
[16] Olmstead 51-52, 57-58.
[17] Omstead 53.

Chapter 5

[1] In fact, as Finkelstein makes clear, the creators of the biblical record were so eager to enhance the reputation of Solomon that many of the grand buildings that had been constructed during the "wicked" Omride monarchy were attributed to him. As the Bible was written a good many years after the completion of these projects, it isn't clear whether this was done intentionally or, rather, was an honest mistake. See Israel Finkelstein and Neil A. Silberman, *The Bible Unearthed* (New York, NY: The Free Press, 2001) 168-195.

[2] Finkelstein and Silberman 231-238.

[3] Norman Rufus Colin Cohn, "Biblical Origins of the Apocalyptic Tradition," *The Apocalypse and the Shape of Things to Come*, ed. Frances Carey (Toronto: University of Toronto Press, 1999) 28.

[4] Cohn, "Biblical Origins of the Apocalyptic Tradition" 31-32.

[5] Cohn, "Biblical Origins of the Apocalyptic Tradition" 32.

[6] Cohn, "Biblical Origins of the Apocalyptic Tradition" 32.

[7] Cohn, "Biblical Origins of the Apocalyptic Tradition" 32.

[8] Cohn, "Biblical Origins of the Apocalyptic Tradition" 33.

[9] Cohn, "Biblical Origins of the Apocalyptic Tradition" 33-34.

[10] Cohn, "Biblical Origins of the Apocalyptic Tradition" 34.

Chapter 8

[1] Marcus J. Borg, *Jesus: Uncovering the Life, Teachings, and Relevance of a Religious Revolutionary* (New York, NY: HarperSanFrancisco, 2006) 66-67.

[2] Borg 68.

[3] Borg 252.

[4] Donald H. Akenson, *Surpassing Wonder: The Invention of the Bible and the Talmuds* (Montreal: McGill-Queen's University Press, 1998) 180.

[5] Borg 19, 44, 307. Here I might add that Borg deviates from traditional earlier scholarship in his interpretation of these elements of the synoptic texts. Earlier scholars tended to interpret "life of the age to come" as life in heaven. They also tended to associate eternal life with heaven.

[6] Tom Harpur, *The Pagan Christ: Recovering the Lost Light* (Toronto: Thomas Allen Publishers, 2004) 37. Of course, Harpur goes much further than illustrating similarities between Christ as presented in the Gospels and saviors in the Pagan tradition. He argues that the Gospels dealing

with the life of Jesus are "essentially religious dramas used for worship and as a form of evangelism." This fits in with Harpur's larger argument that the story of Jesus is essentially a dramatization through one person of accounts already found and described in ancient mythologies relating to the gods, in particular those of ancient Egypt. He makes a good case for his point of view, presenting many parallels between the biblical account of the life of Jesus as found in the Gospels and earlier Pagan mythologies. Furthermore, one cannot quibble with his argument that the Bible is essentially didactic rather than historical in purpose, or with his suggestion that the true meaning of the biblical text is to be found beneath the surface.

Nevertheless, the main thrust of Harpur's argument, namely that Jesus never was a real person but the leading personage of a morality play, does raise certain problems. Looking at the biblical record and Harpur's criticism thereof, one can't escape the conclusion that at least some of the followers of Christ believed that in the case of Jesus they were dealing with an actual man. Furthermore, Harpur's suggestion that the absence of any authoritative proof that Jesus of Nazareth actually existed does not necessarily lead to the conclusion that Christ was therefore a dramatic personage. Except for major world figures whose actions are described in a variety of sources, we would have difficulty saying with absolute certainty that any specific person actually ever existed. This would be true in particular of a person who for a very short period preached and did miracles at the edges of an imperial empire, which Judea was at the time of the Romans. Nor is Harpur's reliance on archeological and other evidence as unassailable a support for his argument as he appears to assume. As I show in my discussion of the archeological evidence as it relates to the conquest account, archaeology may serve a useful function in showing the limitations of the biblical account. However, problems arise when people, after dismissing the biblical record, present to us their particular alternative account.

In this regard, there appear to be more plausible explanations for the presence of Pagan examples in the miracles and sayings of Jesus as presented in the Gospels than one that seeks to establish Christ as the leading figure in a morality play. From the sources at our disposal, we can well conclude that some of the disciples believed Christ to have been of divine origin. We know that they sought to disseminate this belief among Jews and Gentiles. We also know that the actual account of Jesus' life and activities were recorded a good number of years after His death and resurrection. Pagan sources could well have been introduced as the disciples sought to explain Christ, His life and His meaning for humanity to themselves, to the Jewish community, and to the Pagan world around them. This information was then included in the accounts when they were committed to written form a good many years after Christ's death. The Church, through its persecutions and its attacks on Paganism, may have destroyed people's awareness of the original sources on which the sayings and deeds were based. However, it retained those elements in the record that the early followers of Christ added to Scripture to make Christ, His life, and purpose comprehensible to both themselves and others.

In any case, I see Harpur's argument that Christ was in essence a lead figure in a morality play historicized in large part through persecutions by the Church as not really affecting the basic thrust of my argument. Harpur points out the basic similarity between the miracle works of Christ and Pagan deities to show that many of the miracles performed by Jesus, as well as His parables, had their antecedents in Egyptian mythology. He deals little with the broader Christian message of salvation as developed in the New Testament, which is that each individual be aware of his or her thoughts and actions, for these will determine on the judgment day following the final victory of good over evil, whether one is destined for heaven or hell. The basic thrust of this message is found, not in ancient Egyptian mythologies, but in Zoroastrianism.

[7] Harpur 85.

[8] James Barr, "The Question of Religious Influence: The Case of Zoroastrianism, Judaism, and Christianity," *Journal of the American Academy of Religion* (March 1985) 204; Mary Boyce, *Zoroastrians: Their Religious Beliefs and Practices* (London: Routledge & Kegan Paul, 1979).

[9] Barr 219.

[10] Edwin M.Yamauchi, *Persia and the Bible* (Grand Rapids, MI: Baker Book, 1996) 446.

[11] Yamauchi 464-465.

[12] Harpur 133.

[13] W. G. Lambert, *Babylonian Wisdom Literature* (Oxford: Carendon Press, 1960) 59.

[14] See, for example, Akenson, *Surpassing Wonder* 244-269.

[15] Here I might add that the early Christian attempt to assert their legitimate claim to the salvation promised through the God of Abraham helped to lay the basis for Christian anti-Semitism. In some respects, of course, the prophets helped them in this. Citing the different arguments the prophets had used to encourage the Jews to not lose faith in their God, early Christians presented these as proof of Jewish perfidy, which culminated in their crucifying Christ rather than accepting him as savior. Such negative reasoning not only helped lay the base for the new religion but also served to present the Jews as the rejected of God in favour of the new "elect."

[16] Akenson, *Surpassing Wonder* 211-294.

Conclusion
   [1] Borg, 30-76, 265-292, 303-304.

Bibliography

Akenson, Donald H. *Surpassing Wonder: The Invention of the Bible and the Talmuds*. Montreal: McGill-Queen's University Press, 1998.

_____. *Saint Paul: A Skeleton Key to the Historical Jesus*. Montreal: McGill-Queen's University Press, 2000.

Albright, William F. *The Archaeology of Palestine*, revised ed. Harmondsworth, Middlesex: Penguin Books, 1956.

Anderson, Bernard W. *Understanding the Old Testament*. Englewood Cliffs, NJ: Prentice Hall, 1957.

Auld, A. Graeme. *Joshua Retold: Synoptic Perspectives*. Edinburgh: T&T Clark, 1998.

Baez-Camargo, Gonzalo. *Archaelogical Commentary on the Bible*. New York: Doubleday & Co., 1984.

Barr, James. "The Question of Religious Influence: The Case of Zoroastrianism, Judaism, and Christianity." *Journal of the American Academy of Religion* (March 1985): 201-235.

Bauer, Yehuda. *The Holocaust in Historical Perspective*. Seattle: University of Washington Press, 1978.

_____. *A History of the Holocaust*. New York: Franklin Watts, 1982.

Ben-Sasson, H.H., ed. *A History of the Jewish People*. Cambridge, MA.: Harvard University Press, 1976.

Berquist, Jon L. *Judaism in Persia's Shadow*. Minneapolis: Fortress Press, 1995.

Boling, G. et al. *Joshua: A New Translation with Notes and Commentary*. New York: Douleday, 1982.

Borg, Marcus J. *Jesus: Uncovering the Life, Teachings, and Relevance of a Religious Revolutionary*. New York, NY: HarperSanFrancisco, 2006.

Boyce, Mary. *Zoroastrians: Their Religious Beliefs and Practices*. London: Routledge & Kegan Paul, 1979.

Carey, Frances, ed. *The Apocalypse and the Shape of Things to Come*. Toronto: University of Toronto Press, 1999.

Carter, George William. *Zoroastrianism and Judaism,* reprint from 1918 ed. New York, NY: AMS Press, 1970.

Chamoux, François. *The Civilization of Greece*, trans. W.S. Maguinnes. New York: Simon & Schuster, 1965.

Bibliography

Cohn, Norman Rufus Colin. *The Pursuit of the Millennium: Revolutionary Millenarians and Mystical Anarchists of the Middle-Ages.* Rev. and expanded ed. London: Maurice Temple Smith, 1970.

_____. "Biblical Origins of the Apocalyptic Tradition." *The Apocalypse and the Shape of Things to Come.* Ed. Frances Carey. Toronto: University of Toronto Press, 1999. 28-41.

Collins, Adela. "Mark and His Readers: The Son of God among Greeks and Romans." *Harvard Theological Review* 93:2 (April 2000): 85-100.

Collins, John J. *The Apocalyptic Imagination: An Introduction to Jewish Apocalyptic Literature*, 2nd ed. Grand Rapids, MI: William B. Eerdmans, 1998.

Conquest, Robert. *The Great Terror: A Reassessment.* Edmonton: The University of Alberta Press, 1990.

Cook, J. M. *The Persian Empire.* London: J.M. Dent & Sons, 1983.

Cotterell, Arthur, ed. *The Encyclopedia of Ancient Civilizations.* London: Macmillan, 1983.

Craigie, Peter C. *The New International Commentary on the Old Testament: The Book of Deuteronomy.* Grand Rapids, MI.: William B. Eerdmans, 1976.

_____. *The Old Testament: Its Background, Growth and Content.* Burlington, ON: Welch Publishing, 1986.

Davies, Philip. "What separates a Minimalist from a Maximalist? Not much." *Biblical Archaeology Review* 26:2 (March/April 2000): 27-27, 72-73.

De Coulanges, Fusel. *The Ancient City: A Study on Religion, Laws, and Institutions of Greece and Rome.* Garden City, New York: Doubleday, 1956.

Dever, William G. "Archaeology and the Emergence of early Israel." *Archaeology and Biblical Interpretation.* Ed. John R. Bartlett. London and New York: Routledge, 1997. 20-50.

_____. "Archaeology, Syro-Palestinian and Biblical." *The Anchor Bible Dictionary*, vol. 1. Ed. David Noel Freedman et al. New York: Doubleday, 1992. 354-367.

_____. "Archaeology and the Israelite 'Conquest.'" *The Anchor Bible Dictionary*, vol. 3. Ed. David Noel Freedman et al. New York: Doubleday, 1992. 545-558.

Dicks, Brian. *The Ancient Persians: How they lived and worked.* North Pomfret, VT: David & Charles, 1979.

Fine, John V.A. *The Ancient Greeks: A Critical History.* Cambridge, MA: Harvard University Press, 1983.

Finkelstein, Israel and Neil A. Silberman. *The Bible Unearthed.* New York, NY: The Free Press, 2001.

Garlan, Yvon. *War in the Ancient World: A Social History*. Trans. Janet Lloyd. New York: W.W. Norton, 1975.

Good, E.M. "Joshua, Book of." *The Interpreter's Dictionary of the Bible: An Illustrated Encyclopedia*. Ed. G.A. Buttrick. New York: Abingdon Press, 1962. 988-996.

Grant, Michael. *The World of Rome*. London: Readers Union, Weidenfeld & Nicolson, 1962.

Grayson, A.K. "Assyria." *The Encyclopedia of Ancient Civilizations*. Ed. Arthur Cotterell. London: Macmillan, 1983. 101-109.

Gurney, O.R. "The Hittites." *The Encyclopedia of Ancient Civilizations*. Ed. Arthur Cotterell. London: Macmillan, 1983. 111-115.

Hinnells, John R. "Zoroastrian Saviour Imagery and its Influence on the New Testament." *Numen* 16 (1969): 161-185.

_____. "Zoroastrian Influence on the Judaeo-Christian tradition." *Journal of the K.R. Cama Oriental Institute*. Ed. N.D. Minochehr-Homji et al. Bombay: Kaiser-E-Hind Press, 1976.

Hryshko, Wasyl. *The Ukrainian Holocaust of 1933*. Ed. and trans. Marco Carynnyk. Toronto: Bahriany Foundation, 1983.

Hughes, Pennethorne. *Witchcraft*. Harmondsworth, Middlesex: Penguin, 1965.

Jastrow, Morris. *The Civilization of Babylonia and Assyria: Its Remains, Language, History, Religion, Commerce, Law, Art, and Literature*. First publ. 1915. Reissued 1971. New York, NY: Benjamin Blom, 1971.

Kalman, M. "Archaeologist tries to rip out Jewish history's biblical roots," *USA Today* 3 November 1999: 11D.

Katz, Steven. *The Holocaust in Historical Context. Vol. I: The Holocaust and Mass Death before the Modern Age*. New York: Oxford University Press, 1994.

Kenyon, Kathleen M. *Archaeology in the Holy Land*. London: Ernest Benn, 1960.

Kluger, H.V. *Satan in the Old Testament*. Evanston, IL: Northwestern University Press, 1967.

Koester, Helmut. "The Memory of Jesus' Death and the Worship of the Risen Lord." *Harvard Theological Review* 4 (1998): 335-50.

Kramer, Samuel Noah. *The Sumerians: Their History, Culture, and Character*. Chicago: The University of Chicago Press, 1963.

Lambert, W.G. *Babylonian Wisdom Literature*. Oxford: Clarendon Press, 1960.

Larner, Christina. "Crimen Exceptum? The Crime of Witchcraft in Europe." *Witch-Hunting in Early Modern Europe*, vol. 3. Ed. Brian P. Levack. New York: Garland, 1992. 79-105.

Lehmann, Johannes. *The Hittites: People of a Thousand Gods*. Trans. J. Maxwell Brownjohn. New York: The Viking Press, 1977.

Bibliography

Manuel, Frank E. and Fritzie P. Manuel. *Utopian Thought in the Western World*. Cambridge, MA: Harvard University Press, 1979.

Marshall, John W. *Parables of War: Reading John's Jewish Apocalypse*. Kitchener, Waterloo: Wilfrid Laurier University Press, 2001.

Neusner, Jacob. *Judaism, Christianity, and Zoroastrianism in Talmudic Babylonia*. Lanham, MD: University Press of America, 1986.

_____. *Judaism and Zoroastrianism at the Dusk of Late Antiquity: How Two Ancient Faiths Wrote Down their Great Traditions*. Atlanta, GA: Scholars Press, 1993.

Nicholson, E.W. *Deuteronomy and Tradition*. Oxford: Basil Blackwell, 1967.

Niditch, Susan. *War in the Hebrew Bible: A Study in the Ethics of Violence*. New York: Oxford University Press, 1993.

Nigosian, S.A. *The Zoroastrian Faith: Tradition and Modern Research*. Montreal: McGill-Queen's University Press, 1993.

Olmstead, A. *History of the Persian Empire*. Chicago: University of Chicago Press, 1948.

_____. *History of Assyria*. Chicago: University of Chicago Press, 1951.

Olson, Theodore. *Millennialism, utopianism, and progress*. Toronto: University of Toronto Press, 1982.

Roux, Georges. *Ancient Iraq*, 2nd. ed. Harmondsworth, Middlesex: Penguin Books, 1980.

Smith, Morton. "II Isaiah and the Persians." *Journal of the American Oriental Society* 83/4 (1963): 415-421.

Strobel, Lee. *The Case for Christ: A Journalist's Personal Investigation of the Evidence for Jesus*. Grand Rapids, MI: Zondervan, 1998.

Thompson, Thomas L. *The Mythic Past: Biblical Archaeology and the Myth of Israel*. London: Random House, 1999.

Warmington, B.H. *Carthage*. London: Robert Hale, 1980.

Weber, Eugen. *Apocalypses: Prophecies, Cults and Millennial Beliefs Through the Ages*. Toronto: Random House of Canada, 1999.

Wood, Bryant. "Did the Israelites conquer Jericho? A new look at the archaeological evidence." *Biblical Archaeology Review*. 16: 2 (1990): 44-58.

Woolley, C. Leonard. *The Sumerians*. New York: W.W. Norton, 1965.

Yamauchi, Edwin M. *Persia and the Bible*. Grand Rapids, MI: Baker Books, 1990.

Index

Abraham, 27, 33, 34, 72, 77, 102
Achan, son of Carmi, 108
Adam and Eve, 28
Ahab, King of Israel, 54, 76, 77
Ahaz of Judah, 55
Ahriman, 99-101, 106
Ahura Mazda, 99-101, 106, 108
Ai, destuction of, 20
Akenson, Donald H., 111
Alexander of Macedonia, 47, 79, 105
Amelekites, 74
Amorites, 25, 75
Animal sacrifice, 102
Antichrist, 14, 38, 91
Antiochus IV Ephiphanes, 48, 79, 100
Apocalypse, 98, 111
Apocalypse - views of Amerindian, 98; Babylonian, 98; Greek, 98; Nordic, 98; Zoroastrian, 98, 99
Armageddon, 35, 36, 38
Asa, King of Judah, 54
Assyrians, 23, 26, 46, 55-58
Assyrians - view of sin and punishment, 57
Athenians, 24

Baasha, 54
Babylonian god - Marduk, 18, 61, 62, 89, 107
Babylonians, 18, 26, 46, 47, 57, 60, 86, 107

Babylonians - destruction of Jerusalem, 86
Barr, James, 104
Beast, 35, 36
Belief and morality, 37, 38
Ben-Hadad of Syria, 54
Borg, Marcus, 100, 101, 116
Boyce, Mary, 104

Canaan - conquest of, 45
Canaanites, 25
Carthage, destruction of, 24, 25
Child sacrifice, 102
Christ the Messiah, 32, 87, 88, 95, 111
Christ the Savior, 14, 87, 88, 90, 102, 109, 111, 118, 121, 122
Christ the slain lamb, 35, 36, 38, 39
Christ the Son of God, 14, 34, 100, 102
Christ - changing view of, 117, 118
Christian Church, 36
Christians - persecution of, 49, 50
Cohn, Norman Rufus Colin, 107
Covenant, 19, 71, 86
Crucifixion, 100, 109, 110
Cyrus II of Persia, 46, 59-61, 77, 89, 119

Daniel, Book of, 32, 48, 78-80, 88, 90, 103, 107, 120
David, King of Israel, 45, 74, 75, 78, 90, 94
Day of Judgment, 106, 110

Index   143

De Coulanges, Fustel, 24
Debir, destruction of, 22
Defeat and punishment, 63, 64
Dragon, 36

Eglon, destruction of, 21
Egyptians, 19, 20, 35, 55
Egyptian gods -
  Horus, 103, 107; Osiris, 103
Elam, 56
Eleazar, 102
Elect, 12, 13, 27, 32, 36,38, 40, 82, 83, 88, 89, 95, 114-116, 118-120, 123
Elijah, 76, 107, 120
Elisha, 76, 87, 107, 120
Emperor worship, 31, 48, 50, 79
Enoch, Book of, 91
Eternal judgment, 90
Eternal life, 82
Everlasting kingdom, 80

Faithful remnant, 87, 88
Final Judgment, 33-36
Finkelstein, Israel, 77
First Temple, Jerusalem, 75, 78

Garden of Eden, 28
Gentiles, 65, 82, 87, 89, 90, 94, 101, 106, 114, 121
Gezer, destruction of, 21
Gibeonites, 22
Gideon, 86
God and humanity, 27, 36-38, 69, 70, 93
God and gods, 61, 62
God and war gods, 118, 119
God's actions - interpretation of, 115, 116, 118-120
God - biblical view of, 70
God - involvement in warfare, 20-22, 25, 73
God's action and power needs, 123
Greeks, 23

Harpur, Tom, 103, 134-136
Hasmonean family, 48
Hazael, king of Syria, 77, 86
Hazor, destruction of, 20
Heaven, 33, 37, 39, 109, 114, 118
Hebron, destruction of, 21
Hell, 33, 35, 36, 38, 90, 95, 103, 108, 109, 114, 118
Hellenism, 105
Herod (the Great), 49
Herod's Temple - destruction of, 103
History and faith - reconciling their relationship, 124-127
Hittites, 23, 25, 26, 74
Hivites, 25, 74
Holocaust, 13, 17, 26, 27, 29, 114, 115, 122
Holy Land, 17, 18, 26, 27, 37-39, 73, 78, 85, 89, 94, 106, 111, 113,114, 116, 118
Hosea, 100
Hoshea, King of Samaria, 56
Humanity - biblical view of, 69, 70, 113, 114, 122

Idolaters - destruction of, 26-29, 28, 72, 73, 114, 116
Idolatry, 31, 79
Isaac, 86
Isaiah, Book of, 63-66, 77, 78, 119
Israelite traditional concepts of death, 84, 88
Israelite traditional saviors, 88, 89
Israelite war god, 90
Israelites, deportation of, 56

Jacob, 72, 86
Jebusites, 25
Jehoash, King of Israel, 86
Jehoiakem of Judah, 59
Jehu (son of Omri), King of Israel, 55
Jericho, destruction of, 20, 73

Index

Jeroboam, 54
Jerusalem, destruction of, 59, 77, 115
Jesus - crucifixion of, 49
Jewish uprising against Romans, 50
Jews – expulsion to Babylon, 77
Jews - persecution of, 48, 50, 79, 82
Jews - role in the world, 64, 65
Jezebel, Queen of Israel, 77
Job, Book of, 71, 72, 108
Joel, 99
John, author of Book of Revelation, 31-35
Joshua, 20-22, 25, 90, 95, 114
Josiah, King of Judah, 56
Judean War, 31
Judges, Book of, 73
Justice and righteousness, 83

Kingdom of God, 32, 34, 83, 101, 117, 118

Lachish, destruction of, 21
Libnah, destruction of, 21
Lüdemann, Gerd, 23
Luke, Gospel of, 101, 116

Maccabean uprising, 80
Maccabees, 102
Magis, 110
Makkedah, destruction of, 21
Malians, 24
Mark, Gospel of, 101, 116
Marshall, John, 31, 32
Matthew, Gospel of, 101, 116
Medes, 59
Messiah, 93, 94, 101
Midians, 73, 85
Moabites, 23
Monotheism, 8, 12, 17, 18, 26, 28

Nabonidus of Babylon, 59

Nabopolassar of Babylon, 56, 57
Nahash the Ammonite, 74
Nebuchadnezzar of Babylon, 46, 57-59, 77, 89
Nebuchadnezzar's dream, 80
Nehemiah, 47, 103
Neo-Babylonian kingdom, 56
New Jerusalem 2, 13, 35, 37, 95, 111, 114
Nineveh, destruction of, 57
Noah, 69, 110

Pagan Christ, 103
Pagan empires, 82, 83
Pahlavi texts, 105
Paradise, 27, 28, 39, 70, 114, 118, 119
Perizzites, 25, 75
Persians, 46, 59-61, 77, 103, 104
Pharaoh Necho II, 58
Pharisees, 49, 100, 109
Philistine god - Baal, 76
Philistines, 75
Polytheism, 17, 18, 26, 28, 31
Prophets - role of, 75-77
Ptolomies, 47, 48
Punic Wars, 24

Remnant of Jews, 41
Resurrection, 33-36, 84, 90, 103, 107-109
Reward or punishment,18, 25-27, 33-37, 63-65, 70-76, 82-84, 88-90, 95, 97, 106-109, 112-114, 118-122
Reward or punishment - changing nature of, 114
Reward or punishment - eternal, 82-84, 88-90
Reward or Punishment - in time and space, 72-74, 85, 86, 88-90
Righteous remnant, 64, 65, 66, 78, 82, 83, 104, 106
Roman emperors -

Caesar Augustus, 100; Constantine, 50; Domitian, 31, 50; Julius Caesar, 31; Nero, 31
Romans, 24-25, 31, 48-50
Roux, Georges, 54

Sadducees, 109
Saints, 82
Salvation, 34, 35, 38, 39, 87, 95, 109, 110, 117, 118, 120-122
Salvation - changing nature of, 117, 118, 120-122
Samson, 73, 86
Samuel, 88
Satan, 32, 36-38, 95
Saul, King of Israel, 74, 75
Savior, 65, 73, 85-87, 94-95
Savior - of the House of David, 86, 87
Second Temple period, 103, 104, 109
Second Temple, Jerusalem, 47, 101
Seleucids, 47, 80, 88
Seneca, 98
Shalmaneser V of Assyria, 55, 56
Sheol, 84
Sin and punishment, 57, 63, 64, 119, 120
Sins of the people of Judah, 63, 64
Sodom and Gomorrah, 107
Solomon, King of Israel, 45, 54, 101
Son of God, 100, 101

Son of Man savior, 87
Son of Man, 32-34, 81, 82, 87, 90, 91, 94, 115, 117
Sons of the living God, 100
Sumerians, 23, 26
Suptuagint, 47
Syrian god - Baal Shamen, 79

Temporal Jerusalem, 35
Thucydides, 24
Tiglathpileser II of Assyria, 56
Time - changing view of, 115

Utopia, 1, 38, 114

Victory and defeat – explanation of, 62, 63
Virgin birth, 100

War and conquest - changing nature of, 116

Yadin, Yigael, 6
Yamuachi, Edwin M., 105

Zachariah, Book of, 34, 99, 103
Zedekiah, 46
Zerubbabel, 47
Zimri, 54
Zoroastrian savior, 98, 99
Zoroastrianism, 9, 101-108, 110, 114, 116, 121
Zoroastrianism, Judaism and Christianity, 103-108, 110

www.ingramcontent.com/pod-product-compliance
Lightning Source LLC
Chambersburg PA
CBHW032050150426
43194CB00006B/479